Angels on the Roof

by Ilene Smith

Forward Movement Publications, Cincinnati

The author lives in upper New York state deep in the heart of the rural countryside she loves. She is a graduate of Cornell University with a degree in botany and natural sciences. Forward Movement published her first book, *Peace in the Meadow and other encounters with life*. She also contributed the December, 1986, and January, 1987, meditations for *Forward Day by Day*.

Most of her work over the years has been farm related—maintaining a small dairy herd, raising strawberries and vegetables for sale, and making maple sugar. Her life now is centered in a small cabin where she lives and through her writing expresses her deep reverence for God and love of the wild and not-so-wild outdoor places.

Drawings for Angels on the Roof are by Cathy Applegate of Cincinnati.

Most Bible quotations are from the *Good News Bible, the Bible in Today's English Version*, © The American Bible Society.

©1990, Forward Movement Publications, 412 Sycamore Street, Cincinnati, Ohio 45202-41

Introduction

Usually I can be found close to my Bittersweet Garden home deep in the heart of the Northern New York countryside that I love. I would not want to miss the months of winter when the light of a late dawn touches the snowy hillsides with a brief, rosy glow. And I need to be here when opossum stops by for a sweet yellow apple ("Comfort me with apples!") and a peanut butter sandwich to see him through the below-zero nights.

Or the exciting days of springtime when the maple sap is running and something should really be done about it, such as "doing a little sugaring," as the old-timers called it. The hot days of summer come and my herb gardens need attention, weeding and digging and snipping off fragrant bits of dill and sage, catnip, thyme and lavender to dry for use next winter. Finally, breath-taking autumn. The bittersweet comes into its own now. The pale golden husks split open, disclosing the lovely surprise of the scarlet fruits inside. The vines are spectacular as they climb toward October's blazing blue sky.

And so I write something of my life in the "real country," hoping that somehow we can save our endangered earth. I am sure God loves with a "forever love" the beaver babies that swim and play in their sparkling pond waters, the blue gentians in the wet meadows, the snow geese that follow the seasons through the skies, and all other creatures in this beautiful world.

Ilene Smith
Autumn, 1990

Along A Woods' Road

On a dusky winter's day when the brassy smell of snow was in the air, my woodsman friend was entertaining Lira and me in his well-appointed little woods' cabin. Lira had been supplied with a friedcake and I was enjoying a plate of beans. The beans were just Campbell's pork and beans heated up in a battered saucepan on the old woodstove that was sending out awesome waves of welcome heat. They were very good.

Everyone was comfortable and ready for a good in-depth discussion which our host started off by announcing in a challenging way that he had lost his faith and no longer believed in God, the reason being that everywhere he looked in the world he saw crime, poverty, homelessness, disease, death and other calamities. Even though I had just completed a book of religious meditations I could not think of anything to say to refute his claims. I did vaguely think that he was leaving out a few things such as his recovery after hospitalization for a serious heart problem, a family he dearly loves, and this tree farm where he can spend his spare time out among the fragrant pines and spruces. But I could not marshal all of this into a coherent theological discourse. It is a big subject to throw at a hungry person over a dishful of beans. I, too, know that life is full of minefields. Indeed, Lira, my beloved border collie, sleeping now at my feet, is a reminder that we do lose the things we treasure the most. She is 14 years old, with painfully swollen arthritic joints, some heart and breathing problems, and cataracts on her eyes. Some day before long the loving glow in the golden brown eyes that have regarded me with such faithful trust all of these years when I have been alone, is going to dim and go out. I am no stranger to trouble.

Although I understood his feelings, I still felt that they missed the point somehow. But I could not seem to organize a coherent response to my friend's calamitous loss of faith, and he drifted on to other things including the road that he had "swamped out" through his wooded acres during the summer. Before long he was telling about the "pat-ridge" (Northern New York for par-tridge) that he came face to face with while working on his road one day in the springtime, when the young beech leaves were hanging like gauzy wands in the warm sunshine and the small, sparkly white flowers of the dutchman's-breeches brightened up little nooks in the deep ravines.

It seems that the "pat-ridge" was standing on a stump and every feather was all fluffed out and his comb was standing straight up, making the little bird appear two or three times as large as his real size. "His wings were dragging on the stump and he was all set to fly at me," my host complained, with a hint of grudging amusement in his voice. "What did you do?" I asked. "I backed off," was the reply. "I wasn't going to get hit in the face by some gol-danged pat-ridge." "Well, there you are," I said calmly, and encouragingly. "What do you mean there I are, uh, er, there I am?" he demanded, getting his verbs straightened out, but beginning to get a little choleric, as he sometimes does in these discussions. "That would have been a male partridge you saw. He was protecting his mate and their nest full of eggs which must have been close by on the woods' floor. Some One put love and faith and endless courage into the heart of that little bird. For all he knew you might have blasted him to bits with a gun, but it did not stop him. You see, his love was so great. . ." "Oh," my friend replied, and after a long pause he added, "I see what you mean."

Since it was beginning to look like a weather breeder outside, I said goodbye and Lira and I headed homeward along a track that was beginning to fill in with blowing snow. But it was so familiar to us that we easily followed it all the way home to our own welcome fireside.

All the animals in the forest are mine and the cattle on thousands of hills. All the wild birds are mine and all living things in the field.

Psalm 50:10-11

New Shoes for Christmas

After I graduated from high school I took my first year of college at a small institution in the foothills of New York State's Catskill Mountains. When Christmas approached, I went into a local department store to spend some hard-earned babysitting money for family gifts. And here I noticed a little episode that still makes me glad today, about 45 years later.

A farmer had come in with his two boys, about seven and ten years of age, and was inquiring of a very supercilious young salesman about new shoes for his boys. They were to be Christmas presents, he carefully explained.

I knew that life could be pretty hard back on the small subsistence farms in the hills, and there was usually a discouraging shortage of cash. The three were not well dressed. Their overalls and jackets were shabby and had been worn so thin in places that some neat patching had been done in an attempt to hold the garments together. Also there was a penetrating odor of "barn" about their persons.

In those days the stables had to be shoveled out by hand. The manure was heaped in a big pile by the barn to be spread over the fields when the weather was right or when there was time. (A little of this aging manure mixed into some ordinary dirt was the secret of the spectacular, colorful geraniums that many a hill housewife kept in her kitchen windows.) Indoor plumbing and running water were uncommon. Baths and laundering were not embarked upon lightly. And so it is not surprising that

4

sometimes the aroma of sheep and cows, calves and chickens clung to those responsible for their care.

The salesman looked over his would-be customers, barely subduing a sneer, and asked what sizes the boys took. The father didn't know—just a larger size than what they had, which were broken down, scuffed, had holes in them, and were too small. The salesman, raising an eyebrow and winking at a co-worker, said, "Well, we don't have anything to fit them." "You don't?" asked the father anxiously, "but there's all those shoes over there," and he pointed at endless boxes of shoes on the shelves. "We don't have anything to fit them," the salesman repeated and, as the discouraged little group turned to leave, he held his nose mockingly so the other store personnel could see how offensive the good earthly odors of the barn were to him.

This whole episode left me heartsick and I must admit that I wished various calamities might occur to the salesman, and soon. But I could not think of anything to do to set matters right.

The shoe affair was not over, however. I had not been the only one to notice this little family and their shopping problems. A very stout woman, with a cane, a plain black cloth coat, and a velvet pillbox hat jammed down over her ears shouted sternly to the errant clerk, "George, how about these shoes right here—seems as though they'd be just right for these little guys. All sizes, too—you'll never get anywhere in this business, George, if you don't learn your stock and MIND THE STORE, as I always told my late husband who, if I do say so, had the best meat market in town. Reminds me, we're having boiled New England dinner at the Franklin House tonight. Plenty for those who've put in a good day's work, not much though for slackers." This was a serious threat to George, who ate at her boarding house. I later learned that there was always a long waiting list of people who wanted to take their meals at her establishment.

The woman managed to get George actually anxious to locate sturdy, well-fitting shoes for the boys. After the shoes were selected, boxed and tied up with stout string, she escorted the man and his boys over to a rack of warm, winter jackets. She said she had just happened to notice that they had been drastically marked down in what she called a pre-Christmas sale, fixing George with a flinty stare. George hastily agreed that this was correct. In the end, the father, with a pleased look on his thin, tired face, and the boys, carefully carrying their purchases, started out of the door. Just then, the lady puffed up to them and dropped a bag of old-fashioned chocolate drops with creamy vanilla centers into one of the sacks. "Little extra, from Santa Claus," she intoned severely. "See that you have a good Christmas now!"

"Well!" I thought, "You just never do know where angels are going to appear." I was at a skeptical age and didn't exactly believe in angels! I had certainly never thought of an angel as being a heavy-set, tightly corseted middle-aged lady, red-faced, with work-worn hands, and over-bearing manner, and hair marcelled in a way that was out of style even back then. And certainly not in a crowded department store full of tired, snappish Christmas shoppers (and clerks). But there it was—my own eyes had seen one.

In the years since, I have seen some other angels. They, too, were quite a revelation to one who had always envisioned them as having flowing robes, gauzy wings and carefully balanced halos! But even though they did not fit into my fanciful notion of angels, they always managed to bring peace, happiness and love into some situations that appeared dead-ended.

Angels On The Roof

One of the things you have plenty of, if you live in lake-effect snow country is....well....SNOW. Snow is a very delightful substance. It caps fenceposts and other rather ordinary objects in a most decorative way. Snow inspired some of Robert Frost's poetry. It spreads a warm, insulating blanket over the fields. This snug covering is beneficial for next season's crops, providing warmth for the roots of plants, as well as moisture, minerals and trace elements. Old-timers were always glad to see plenty of snow and referred to it as "poor man's fertilizer." (They also felt that rocks had a fertilizing value, but then, they were a self-reliant kind of people who made do with what they had!)

Wilson "Snowflake" Bentley of Jericho, Vermont, a great appreciator of snowstorms, spent a lifetime photographing and studying the beauty of snow crystals. The blowing, drifting snow ominously forecast on the radio was a pleasure to Mr. Bentley.

Clean, white snow is a perfect match for the winter color of some animals of the north, such as the snowshoe hare. He loves the deep woods where garlands of ground pine grow on the woods' floor and thick evergreens shut out the bleak winds. In the summertime, arrayed in his soft brown coat, he has been known to enter my dooryard and nip off sweet william and begonia plants.

Beneficial as snow is, however, it sometimes accumulates so heavily on a roof that collapse of the building seems imminent. During the winter of 1977, after a smothering seven-day blizzard, my elderly neighbor finally lost his great barn, which simply folded up one night in silent weariness beneath an incalculable weight of snow.

Built in the 1800s, it had in its day comfortably housed cows, horses, sheep, goats, chickens and some pampered guinea fowl who sat on the windowsills and shrieked in alarm if they noticed any approaching visitors. At the time of its demise, however, the barn was mostly empty, although motes of golden hay and straw dust still floated in the beams of sunlight that stole into the shadowed interior. And it was home to a large number of cats. When the barn sank down in a monumental heap of timbers, old fodder, ancient farming tools and other agricultural impedimenta, a vast dispersal of felines took place over the entire countryside. Weeks afterward they were still showing up at other rural dwellings.

Now, by mid-December, we had already had a winter's worth of winter here in the back country. During the course of several quiet, windless nights, heavy snowfalls deposited a covering four feet deep on my cabin roof. I could hardly bear to think of the strain on the building. I began a search for someone to shovel the roof, a well-known but not greatly sought after occupation around here. I met remarkable apathy concerning my snow-beleaguered home, so finally I decided that I would have to do the job myself. I set a ladder of rather indifferent merit against the building (later on, my nephew inspected the ladder and reported that it was "no good") and then stood there attempting to summon courage to climb it.

Just then a car drove up. Two young women, *Peace In the Meadow* readers, had stopped by to see me. They kindly inquired how I happened to be standing by the ladder holding a shovel. When they heard of my plans for the roof, they glanced at each other, gently removed the shovel from my grasp, and drifted easily up the ladder.

From the roof one of my friends asked me if I had another shovel. I did have one but it had carelessly been left outside and was now hopelessly hidden by the snow. I did find a small spade which I handed up and then I continued to probe the drifts for the missing shovel. In the fall a clerk at a nearly roadside farm market has assured me that we were in for a hard winter—a *really* bad one. His

8

forecast had been based on the unusual thickness of the husks on the ears of sweet corn sold at the stand. If I had been more mindful of her warnings, I might have stored my snow shovels more carefully.

Meanwhile, clouds of snow were being flung down from the roof, and soon, under such a vigorous assault, the snow was all deposited on the ground. "Angels," I whispered to myself in quiet wonder. Angels on the rooftop bringing peace, safety and love to my little storm-battered home. Also, my feeling that angels have an affinity for ladders seemed to be a sustainable idea.

My snow problems were not completely over. During the following days my car, parked in a turnoff near the road, was buried most of the time by drifts and by banks of snow thrown by the snowplows. I shoveled every day but the situation only worsened. Finally, one stormy afternoon I looked out and saw the father of the young people on my old farm clearing the whole area out with a snow scoop attached to his truck. "Angels," I thought. I could see that angels are good with pickup trucks and snow scoops as well as ladders!

God will put his angels in charge of you to protect you wherever you go.
Psalm 91:11

Gifts

Christmas is a lovely time of year here in the northland. There is usually a good supply of snow. Almost everyone hopes for a white Christmas and it is mostly felt that a green Christmas is unnatural, with a disregard for the fact that deep snow was apparently not an outstanding feature of the first Christmas. I always just say that I love a green Christmas, but my friends are tolerant and overlook this statement.

The hard part about Christmas involves the presents that need to be selected or made for our family and friends. Often our perception of what someone else might need or like is flawed and as a result stores are deeply involved in gift exchanges after Christmas Day. However, we do occasionally have the joy of finding a felicitous gift for someone. Price is not necessarily a factor in this process. I think of a recent gift that only cost me twenty-five cents, for it was a discard book picked up at a library book sale.

I have a friend who goes 'way back, to my childhood near the little hamlet of Champion. She collects Gladys Taber books, some of which are almost impossible to find, even through her network of rare and old book dealers. The book I bought was *Mrs. Daffodil.* In a sneaky, roundabout conversation with my friend I found out that she still lacked this book in her collection.

As Christmas approached, I wrapped it up in colorful paper and put it in her gift box, along with one or two more costly items. Immediately after Christmas I received a thank-you note. She wrote that she had been so involved with entertaining family, including the grandchildren, over Christmas, as well as attending church services and serving a holiday dinner, that she had not quieted down. She said that she could hardly believe it when she opened the book package. "I had searched for it so long with no luck. And suddenly I was holding it in my hands."

Another gift, this time for a little wild friend last Christmas, was also well received, I think. I was snowed in and just kept Christmas alone in my cabin, assisted by Lira, my border collie, and Altoona, my cat, both of whom like to be included in festive occasions. Lira, however, soon became tired, falling asleep full of turkey and gravy, which she loves. She was deep in the dreams that old dogs have, resting on the new thick fluffy rug that I had given her just that day. Altoona played a bit with the Christmas tree ornaments, her loving sea-green eyes alight with wonder at the mystery of the little evergreen full of bright colored balls and loops of cranberries that were nice to bat around. No matter that she finally happened to break a popcorn chain and also knocked a tiny angel's halo down around its ears.

But she too went to sleep at last, a gaily colored bag of dried catnip, given to her by a herbalist friend, snugged up against her chest to comfort her while she dreamed and woke and dreamed again.

Meanwhile, I slipped out of the cabin with a pail of windfall apples to see if my culvert muskrat friend was badly snowed in. I found that he had managed to keep several of his plunge holes open and so I dumped the apples down the largest one. It must have been deep for the resulting splash reverberated from such remote depths it was as if I had thrown them into a deep well. Before long a little rumpus in muskrat's watery canals indicated that he had found his gift. I hoped it would be pleasing to him in the heavy snow moon when life can be hard for a housebound muskrat.

Of course, gifts are not restricted to Christmas, and I remember a friend who toured the British Isles last fall. There she was, deep in the homeland of such legendary people as Shakespeare, Dickens, Wordsworth, Cromwell and James Herriott. But the souvenir she brought home for me was a key chain with a colorful picture of Garfield the cat on the wooden tag. She had found it at a craft fair in an English market town, and knew that it was just right for me because I am so fond of Garfield.

Always we remember the perfect gift that God gave to us long ago in Bethlehem. The gift is forever new and comes from the heart of one who knows and loves us, our hopes and dreams, even our inadequacies and failures. And he continues to give us tokens of his love. Just this morning (July 19th), walking under the roadside maple trees, I

11

happened to notice something small and polished lying in the road. Actually it looked like a pearl. Indeed for me it was more precious than a pearl, for closer inspection revealed that it was an empty hummingbird's eggshell. When whole, the little egg had been about the size of a large garden pea, a smooth, off-white color. There must have recently been a second hatch of hummingbird babies nearby. Like many birds, the mother had tucked one half of the shell into the other half and then dropped them some distance from the nest.

I had never seen a hummingbird's egg before and as I held it in my hand it seemed so tiny to have held a living, growing bird. Did God have a problem getting the little hummingbird's long flower-probing beak arranged in the tiny egg? But then, some of God's greatest gifts come in very small packages!

Decorating the Christmas Tree

It had been an old southern planter's house in Virginia and the front hall was mammoth. And so was the doorway through which three men had struggled to bring the Christmas tree. Now it stood there, so perfect, beautiful, mysterious, waiting. Tiny, intricately wrought glass icicles glittered in the fragrant green depths. Expensive imported ornaments of all kinds made it a shimmering, intoxicating pledge of a Christmas in the grand tradition.

The setting for this lovely tree was a home and school for handicapped children where I was working far from my own Northern New York home. I had helped to unwrap the valuable ornaments and place them on the tree. For the rest of the year they were carefully wrapped in fluffy cotton or tissue paper and stored away in the vast attics.

I loved the beautiful tree but felt a little lonesome for the Christmas trees of my own childhood. There were only a few purchased decorations on those trees, but there were lots of somewhat lopsided cardboard bells, faintly misaligned stars, colorful red Santas, and miles of paper chains, pasted together by small, sometimes fumbling fingers. The whole effect, lovingly tolerated by our parents, seemed indescribably marvelous to my brothers and me.

Also, I have always been enchanted by Charlie Brown's doomed search for a perfect Christmas tree. And so, with all this in mind I decided I would find a little tree of my own that needed to belong to someone. I would decorate it using only ornaments I made myself and set it up in my room at the home. It would remind me of days gone by and of our Saviour who breaks through barriers of wealth and poverty, indifference and sin, to bring us peace, hope and a new life in Him at Christmastime.

On my next day off, I took a walk across the icy meadows that belonged to the home. I remembered noticing on previous walks some scrubby little red cedar trees dispersed through the neglected fields. Sure enough, before long I found a small spindly tree about two feet high. It was not very straight and there were empty spaces where the tree had been unable to summon up sufficient energy to grow branches. A perfect Charlie Brown Christmastree! Young red cedars have some real pin-pricking needles, and even with heavy winter gloves I winced as I pulled up the tree. Although the branches were a collection of dubious appendages, the roots were strong and resisted mightily my efforts to separate them from the red clay of Virginia. But, finally, persistent effort paid off and I had my tree.

Now I needed another as I had decided to put one on either side of the fireplace in my room. It was not at all difficult to locate another small tree, equally destitute in appearance. I carried the trees back to the home in a sack. Down in the dark and rather scary cellar I found two flower planters and I placed a little tree in each one and packed gravelly sand around the roots to hold them steady.

The rest of that day, and also the next, I spent considerable time appropriately decorating the trees. The children seemed to know, through some grapevine of their own, that I was preoccupied with an important matter, and were not at all reticent about making inquiries. I finally admitted what I was doing—rather crossly, for after all it was hard work making a Charlie Brown tree, and it had occurred to me that the children might make fun of the enterprise. But the youngsters flocked around like a covey of busy quail, besieging me with demands to let them see the trees.

Finally, I brought down the tree that had been completed and set it in the middle of their library table. Colored pages from magazines had provided the material for a colorful paper chain that spiraled around the tree. Then I had found a full page ad in a lovely shade of yellow, and had used this to cut out two continuous strips of ducks. This is an art which is done by folding a piece of paper many times, and then cutting out the pattern just once. (I usually fold the paper wrong the first time and everything falls apart.) The pattern for the ducks had been taken from an ad for duck decoys in still another magazine. The ducks were covered with printing, and perhaps I should have selected a bird that really does

14

perch in trees. Nevertheless, the small ducks nestled down and looked quite at home among the twigs of the accommodating little tree.

Glittering soap wrappers had been cut and pasted into globular Chinese lanterns. Golden cardboard from a shampoo box had been used to make a star that was now hanging on a bit of thread from the top of the tree. And, rummaging through my belongings, I found several tiny silver keys that had once been used for diaries and suitcases. These were hung on the tree to fill in an empty space or two. These represented the keys of the kingdom. Tiny white crocheted snowflakes hung from several of the branches.

For a moment the children were astonished into complete silence. Then a little boy on crutches wonderingly fingered the sharp needles, and in a practical manner inquired how I had managed to pull up such a prickly tree. The other children gradually revived and, before I knew it, in the beguiling way of children, they succeeded in transferring the ownership of the tree from my hands into theirs. They happily carried it off to their schoolroom, assuring me that they needed it for their classroom Christmas party. The next time I saw the tree, their gifts to each other were piled around it, and a sign propped up nearby explained that this was "Charlie Brown's Christmas Tree."

Out in the main hall there was still the wonderful, mysterious pine, that seemed almost to fill the huge room. A mountain woodsman came on Christmas Eve to pick up his small daughter and take her home for the holidays. He touched the magnificent tree and announced in a hushed voice that this must be a spruce-pine. Spruce-pines are not abundant and are valued more highly than the more common southern pines, such as scrub and pitch pines.

Then, studying the dimensions of the doorway, and those of the tree, he inquired how it had been brought

15

through the doorway. I could not provide any help here, as it seemed like an impossibility to me, also. So we lapsed into a moment's silence. The needles gave off their pungent, fresh odor. Pinpricks of light danced and shone in the remote depths of the tree. And there seemed to be a suggestion that nothing is impossible at Christmastime—kindness, faith, goodwill, and a loving baffling bit of mystery.

You will leave Babylon with joy; you will be led out of the city in peace. The mountains and hills will burst into singing, and the trees will shout for joy.

Isaiah 55:12

Living Low on the Food Chain

Over the years, one of my favorite farm crops has been the dried bean. And, of all the beans, I love the great northern white bean the best. This is an heirloom bean which was first grown by the Mandan Indians of the Missouri River valley and came into general use in other gardens after 1907.

I have been beguiled by other beans—who can help but admire the beauty of the Vermont cranberry bean, the yellow-eye bean, or the wren's egg bean, to name a few. I have dipped my hand into a jar of Jacob's cattle beans and thought of the vicissitudinous life of Jacob, as I let the beans run through my fingers back into the container. And the lovely Christmas lima bean, reminding us of the holy season. There are so many handsome beans available. I can really find nourishment for my dreams in the Vermont Bean Seed Company catalog that carries so many varieties and decorates its pages with exquisite artwork dealing with the bean. To me the Vermont Bean

Seed Company is one of Vermont's great natural resources, like maple syrup, the Vermont common cracker, and the Green Mountains.

Much as I admire all beans, however, I invariably raise the great northern, for it always produces a good crop in the soil that I have here, and the beans always readily cook up to a delectable consistency that makes bean eating a joy. I don't know how that old contemptuous saying, "He's not worth a hill of beans," ever got started; like that famous bean-grower, Henry David Thoreau, I view all my beans as valuable. Thoreau wrote concerning beans, "What shall I learn of beans or beans of me? I cherish them, I hoe them, early and late I have an eye to them; and this is my day's work." I have the same happy feeling about this crop. The soldier-straight rows of plants with velvety dark green leaves, the delicate white blossoms tinged with palest lavender, worked over by hummingbirds, and finally by late August the green pods ripening to a pale tan color. I hasten to pick them before the fall rains set in. All this is a joy to me.

Working with beans has never seemed like work to me, except perhaps one hot August afternoon when I was hurriedly picking rows full of the crisp, fully matured pods before a threatening thunderstorm would have a chance to discolor the beans. A salesman happened along and hopefully suggested that we sit down in some nearby maple shade while he told me about the merits of his products. I told him sternly, "The only way anybody can talk to me today is if they want to get out in this bean patch. I can't stop for anything!" The salesman's interest declined rapidly as he surveyed the blazing hot bean patch, and he soon drove off. This was probably just as well, for I am not really "into" consumerism, and would have been a poor prospect.

It occurred to me that I was harder to talk to than God, for you can talk to God any time, any place. But I think God understood that it would be depressing for me to see

17

those hard lustrous white beans become discolored and marred by being drenched in rainwater. I managed to beat the rainstorm, which was welcome after the beans were safely under cover, spread out on newspapers, laid down on the floor of the empty dairy barn.

Later on in the fall, I go out to the barn, gather up an ancient tin pan full of the pods, and shuck them out in the house. Those dark early evenings and lonesome rattling winds of November and December don't seem nearly so bad when you have a pan of beans to shuck out, considering meanwhile what nutritious food, low in calories, but high in protein and fiber, one is handling. One evening when I was involved in this work, an acquaintance stopped by with her two young daughters. She looked at the bean pods in complete astonishment and asked if that was what beans looked like before they were bagged up and put on the supermarket shelves. And so I realized with a little sadness how completely out of touch the average grocery shopper is with the land and the entire growing cycle. The little girls were quite enthralled with the beans and I guess the whole experience seemed to them almost as good as a school field trip.

Many of my beans are sold, but I keep enough to make baked beans, a good meal for those blizzardy, bone-chilling days of winter. A cup or two of left-over baked beans makes a fine addition to a kettle of homemade beef-vegetable soup, adding a full-bodied mild flavor and serving as the best soup thickener I have ever discovered. I guess there is such a thing as cabin fever up here in the North Country, but with a kettle of this soup, a few good books and some useful handwork to pick up, one can eke out quite a psychologically comfortable existence. God, I am sure, does not want us to find life empty and meaningless, but will help us to live as bravely and well as our hands and hearts allow us to.

As I stir the contents of my own soup kettle I remember gratefully the Mandan Indians who cherished and used these delectable beans so long ago, and passed on the knowledge of their goodness so that latecomers such as myself could also enjoy them.

One day while Jacob was cooking some bean soup, Esau came in from hunting. He was hungry and said to Jacob, "I'm starving; give me some of that red stuff." (That is why he was named Edom.) Jacob answered, "I will give it to you if you give me your rights as the first-born son." Esau said, "All right! I am about to die; what good will my rights do me."

Genesis 25:29-32

Bears on the Back Trail

My childhood days were spent in a time when there was an adage for any situation, such as "Early to bed, early to rise, makes a man healthy, wealthy and wise." Then there were "Don't put all your eggs in one basket," "Cleanliness is next to Godliness" (I thought for many years that this was straight out of the Bible until I discovered that it originated with John Wesley), and that one quoted freely for the benefit of children, braggy relatives, and uppity neighbors, "Pride goeth before a fall." I admit to having my fair share of pride and to prove it I will tell you about my "snowshoe experience."

Even in the harshest, coldest weather I like to go over the frozen brooks, and through fields and woods to see what the wild folk are doing. For many years I accomplished this by using a pair of skis which had been given to one of my brothers in his youth. By some sort of process of default they had been handed down to me. There were no bindings, simply a leather strap that buckled across the foot. A bit of paraffin used occasionally on the skis supposedly made them move across the snow more easily. I had used the skis so much that I was quite skillful at managing them. After many winters the straps disintegrated and I used baler twine to hold the skis on. (I don't think baler twine will catch on.)

Finally, one ski broke and I was grounded. But then I remembered the snowshoes that had been my sister's pride and joy. I had always taken good care of them, in her memory, and perhaps now would be a suitable time to try snowshoeing. After all, country-type magazines often suggest that snowshoeing is the best way to wander over snowy countrysides, and all of those *coureurs d' bois* of the Canadian northlands couldn't have been wrong. To quote an article in one of my favorite magazines, "Snow-shoeing demands neither practice or instruction. If you can walk, you can snowshoe, because that's the only technique required. Snowshoeing is merely the humani-zation of things noted in the animal world, such as the wide, very furry paws of the Snowshoe Rabbit and the little horny comblike projections on the grouse's claws that enable it to easily walk around the winter-locked woods, under snowy spruces and hemlocks in a neatly paced walk."

An article in another magazine, however, made me wonder if this method of locomotion is so problem-free after all. It pointed out that you can't back up; to reverse direction you have to make a U-turn. This can be a really sticky situation if you have absent-mindedly snowshoed to the edge of some steep precipice, such as are quite common in this area. Another useful rule mentioned was, "Do not step out with one snowshoe while standing on it with the other. (Doing this has given more than one novice a faceful of snow.) The acceptable walking tech-nique, according to this writer, is to lift a snowshoed foot, push it forward so that the inner edge of the shoe passes above the inside edge of the shoe still on the ground, coming down far enough ahead to avoid your tripping and falling flat in the snow. The tracks behind one should be in the form of an interlocking chain. The backtrail should be checked frequently. If the prints show side by side, this is not good form unless you are using the narrow Green Mountain bearpaw, with which it is apparently correct to track side by side.

Well, anyway I thought if all of those Scandinavians, Royal Canadian Mounties and so on could do it so easily it must at least be possible. So one very snowy day I fetched the snowshoes down from the spare room and with a good deal of difficulty arranged my feet in the rigging (a mischievous arrangement of straps and buckles that supposedly keeps the snowshoe attached to the foot).Then I set out, and for awhile all went well. No doubt I was experiencing beginner's luck. My backtrail was a little bit sloppy but it didn't look too bad. Then I became busy admiring the snow-laden trees and shrubbery, the tiny sparkling rainbow prisms of the new snowflakes, and thinking what a really healthful, homesteading style of travel this was, when suddenly I found myself falling headfirst into a hidden, snow-filled ditch. My head was pretty well buried in snow, my feet and legs were rather feebly waving around, and every time I attempted to attain an upright position I simply sank in deeper. After quite a few anxious moments I finally managed, with the assistance of my walking stick (a broom handle) to attain an upright position and drag myself out of the hole. I was safe, but I had certainly ruined the lovely tracing of my backtrail. It looked as though a bear had been wallowing around in the snow.

Since that first introduction to snowshoeing I have become a little more adept. I have learned that it is necessary to be careful around ravines, gullies, ditches, deadfalls and snowdrifts—any place where the depth of snow can be deceptive and where there may be varying degrees of hardness in the snow pack.

Not long ago an old-time friend passing through stopped for a short visit. Since he lives in the backwoods of Maine

21

he is quite familiar with outdoor pastimes. He remarked that, living out in the country as I do, I probably found snowshoes to be almost indispensable. "Oh, yes," I agreed brightly. "They're certainly great for getting around." "Well, what kind of snowshoes do you use?" he wanted to know. Hastily casting around in my head for some answer that might at least seem reasonable, I said "Er, they're yukons, I think; uh, no, I guess maybe they're bearpaws. Modified bearpaws," I added hopefully. "Well, let's see them," he said. I produced my snowshoes and to my surprise he touched them reverently and said quietly, "These are Westovers, sometimes called beavertailed bearpaws." He went on to explain that this is the only snowshoe design evolved in the Adirondack Mountain area of New York. And, politely guessing that my snow-shoeing knowledge was not too comprehensive, he told me that this snowshoe was better than an ordinary bearpaw because it does not have the bearpaw's annoy-ing tendency to revolve as you swing it forward on each step.

I do quite a bit of snowshoeing now, keeping a weather-eye out for safety problems in the terrain, and often checking the backtrail to see if it is as pristinely beautiful as I would like it to be.

Unto every one of us is given grace according to the measure of the gift of Christ.

Ephesians 4:7

Lights in the Meadow

I was often asked if I have seen any deer lately and I usually simply look vague and reply, "You know, I hadn't thought about it but I haven't seen any deer in a long time.

Too bad; I love to see them. Maybe they've gone way back in, up on Tug Hill." I have found it best not to gossip too freely about the doings of my wild neighbors!

During the winter months when deer from miles around spread out and feed in the vast cornfields near my cabin, all sorts of people say to me, "Saw a lot of deer in that cornfield near you, back toward the woods. Must have been 60 or 70 anyway. We were up there on our old road yesterday afternoon with the kids, watching them." They say this in sort of an accusing way, hinting that they were outdoors having a good wilderness experience while I must have been in my cabin, huddling by the fire and not "interacting with the environment." I just murmur, "yes, I know," while they tell me more about watching the deer.

I am glad they have this innocent, pleasant pastime available to them, for I, too, watch the deer. I especially love those magical moments when dusk is falling. At first the cornfields seem empty and then, like a picture slowly coming into focus, you see the deer in little groups or singly all over the place. They paw up kernels of golden corn from beneath the snow and feed. Sometimes they raise their white flags and bound back into the woods for awhile if something alarms them. When darkness finally settles in, the Great Dipper, Orion the Hunter, and other bright constellations serve as their lamps for the night hours.

Actually, all through the year I watch the deer when I am able to, but they are elusive and mostly I just have glimpses of them, or note signs of their presence—their delicate crescent-moon shaped hoofprints in the dirt road near the Pond, or a fine rack of shed antlers in the cloistered dimness beneath the pines. There is a brushy wild apple orchard near my cabin and sometimes on winter days I go there just to see the trails the deer have made to the trees where winds straight from the arctic have blown down a new supply of apples, a much cherished deer food. These are very old apple trees and some

23

of the apples are real "keepers," clinging to the trees into late winter. This is fortunate, for it ensures that the harvest for the deer will be spread out through all the cold months.

They also have beds here, deer-sized hollows on the icy ground, where there are flattened soft wispy clumps of last summer's grasses. Many are beneath the pines and spruces too, cushioned by thick spongy layers of dead golden pine needles. They are well shielded from the blizzards that sometimes scour this northern countryside.

I see scrapes, bare places on the ground made by the bucks during the excitement of the fall rutting season, and just recently I saw a leatherwood bush torn and splintered by a buck who had been using it to rub off the velvet from his hardening horns.

Leatherwood is a shrub that loves the streamside banks around here, but I do not think it is common in many places. I had never seen it until we moved to our Rodman farm in 1959. From the first, I admired its velvety brown leaf buds in winter, the small, sunny yellow flowers of the early April woods, the egg-shaped, soft green leaves that turn to pale gold in autumn, and the coral-red berries which quickly disappear because birds admire them, too.

Indians used leatherwood's pliant tough bark for bowstrings, fishlines, and baskets. Deer and moose browse on the leaves and twigs, and deer may use it in autumn as a practice battleground where they can get rid of the itching velvet of their horns, and perhaps vanquish an imaginary rival or two, since mating is on their minds then.

While walking in the winter woods I have sometimes been considerably startled by the blowing noise of a deer. Deer are often considered to be almost voiceless, but if they are disturbed or uneasy they can make a great heaving commotion that carries a long way through the leafless woods of winter.

24

Once on a scorching, humid summer day I scared up a half-grown deer from a little pool in the creek where it had been cooling off. I had thought I was just seeing a bit of straggly branches or roots, caught by a backwash in the shaded waters by an uprooted willow tree, but it all straightened up and arranged itself into a small deer who sped hastily off into the woods. The deer love the rippling creek water and quiet pools as much as I do.

Just once in all of my years among the deer have I seen fawns. They were twins, each curled up under its own wild apple tree. The trees were close together, but separate enough for safety. Fragrant pink and white petals were gently falling on the tiny, motionless deer who watched me with quiet woods-dark eyes, as I carefully backed away so I would not disturb them.

There was also the New Year's Day when, well after dark, the son and daughter of friends who had extended to me a supper invitation were driving me home. It had been a very cold day, with ice underfoot and severe snow squalls earlier in the afternoon, but now the storm had died down. As the car turned into my driveway we saw in the beam of the headlights dozens of golden lights—shifting, turning, dancing—eyeshine from a herd of deer in the meadow beyond the cabin. It was the same glow of golden light I see when the candles at church are burning during the service.

"On wow!" the girl breathed in a hushed, wondering voice, as all three of us quieted, to watch in stillness this lovely sight. And then the shadowy deer wheeled, turned, and bounded off over the ice-crusted meadow.

I feel fortunate that now and then I have these tender, fleeting glimpses into the lives of the beautiful, gentle, graceful white-tail deer.

Living Space

Recently I read in *Country Journal Magazine* a review of "A Place Of Your Own Making," by Stephen Taylor, sub-titled "How To Build a One Room Cabin, Studio, Shack or Shed." The reviewer found the book unique in that it made "absolutely no mention of Henry David Thoreau." I think the reviewer had a point; we Thoreau people do like to drop his name any time there is even a remote chance to insert one of his wonderful thoughts, such as "Why should I feel lonely? Is not our planet in the Milky Way?" This was in answer to statements such as, "I should think you would feel lonesome down there [at Walden Pond] and want to be nearer to folks, rainy and snowy days and nights especially."

One of my favorite writers, the Adirondack Mountains' own Anne LaBastille, wrote in her book *Woods Woman* that ever since a New York City childhood she had wanted to live in a Thoreau-style cabin in the woods. Eventually her dream came true and she built a cabin on what, in the interests of privacy, she calls Black Bear Lake in her beloved Adirondacks. The main indoor room of her cabin is 12 by 12 feet. Thoreau's abode was slightly larger, 10 by 15. However, Anne has an enclosed back porch with an enclosed sleeping loft over it which gave her a little more space than her mentor. Later on she built a second cabin that she called Thoreau II in an even more remote location. It was 10 by 10. This slightly smaller size was necessary in order to meet Adirondack Park Agency regulations.

My own cabin is 12 by 24, divided into two rooms by a partition with a doorway, but no door, as this would take up space, a precious commodity in such a small building. At each end of the cabin there is a small two-sash window, with two panes set in each sash. My writing table is set near the one on the south side of the cabin and here as I read and write I can look out directly into the bird feeder and see how things are going there. All the birds are lovely and interesting and sometimes I see something special, such as the song sparrow last spring who had just one snow white tail feather among the usual brown ones.

Each room also has two small push-out screened windows set high enough in the walls so there is privacy without the need for curtains. Thoreau had no draperies at his Walden Pond cabin as he had "no gazers to shut out but the sun and the moon." When astronomical alignments are correct I, too, can sometimes see the sun, moon and sundry stars from my windows. Also the blueness or storminess of the sky. I look out into the branches of the buckthorn tree on winter days to see the robins, evening grosbeaks, white crowned sparrows and cardinals feeding on the small dark, purple fruits. One stormy day recently a cardinal perched on the outer window sill on the west side spent some time looking thoughtfully into my snug living arrangements. I admired the sunlight shining through his glowing pink bill and reflected that he is the only bird I know of who has a colorful bill to match his fine plumage. He raised and lowered his crest and flicked his tail and seemed to find any home satisfactory. Most of my visitors do seem to approve of my simple life style, although a clergyman friend who stopped by one day said that my condition in life seemed meager to him. Perhaps so, but how can life be truly meager when a cardinal perches on your window sill and when your residence is somewhere in the Milky Way?

Thoreau's cabin, of course, became very famous and there is now a replica of it near Walden Pond. But there is another cabin, sort of a "sleeper" among cabins, that I also love to think about. I have in mind Henry Beston's cabin built at the top of a dune on the outermost beach of Cape Cod where wind, sand and ocean move ceaselessly to shape the coastal world. Eventually he moved to

Maine, where he lived for many years and wrote that lovely book *Northern Farm*. But he spent a year on the Great Beach of Cape Cod writing about his life in that awe-inspiring place. His simple cabin measured 20 by 16 and was divided into two rooms. Considering the incessant gales, storms and blowing sands, I would think he had too many windows to be very cozy—7 in one room and 3 in the other. But he wanted to be a part of life on the Great Beach.

He lived there and wrote *The Outermost House* in 1929. In later years the shifting dunes and encroaching sea made it necessary for the Park Service to build a duplicate of the now famous house in a somewhat more sheltered place. Toward the end of his book he wrote, "Hold your hands out over the earth as over a flame. . .touch the earth, love the earth, honor the earth. . ." What lovely words, as new and bright now as they were years ago when he first wrote them.

For some reason the human heart is especially entranced with small habitations. We do not usually concern ourselves with the exact dimensions of Buckingham Palace or the White House or the Tuileries, but we like to measure a tiny abode and find out just how small a dwelling can be and still serve as a useful beloved home on God's beautiful, flowered, wooded and oceaned earth.

Lord, thou hast been our dwelling place in all generation.
Psalm 90:1

I Didn't Hear a Thing

Once when the Lord spoke to Elijah, the prophet had to wait for awhile and listen very closely, because God did not make himself known in the tumult of the wind, the earthquake or the fire. He spoke in a soft whisper when all was still after the fire. God speaks to us today in many ways, I believe—sometimes in a holy, waiting stillness, but also through the restless, clamoring world that often disturbs our peaceful way of life.

There was my maple sugar business, for instance. A good many maple trees, about thirty, grew along the roadside and in the yard of my beloved old farmhouse where I lived alone for many years. The seasons came and went and it did not occur to me to tap the trees and make maple syrup. I even had a nice sugaring pan bought some years before by my father from the G.H. Grimm Company of Rutland, Vermont, makers of maple sugaring supplies. When we had lived on our Belleville farm, I had helped my father make syrup, but it was something I assumed I could not manage by myself.

Then, late one winter, the neighboring farmer who cut the hay on my meadows eyed me in a kindly, concerned way and said that he'd been thinking that maybe we could do a "little sugarin' together," using my maple trees and sugaring pan. A later discussion revealed that I was to have no actual part in the proceedings. The farmer planned to take the pan to his farm where he would set it up in the yard and undertake the boiling of sap with the assistance of his lively brood of youngsters. For the loan of my sugar trees and pan, I would receive several quarts of syrup. I must say that my pride was hurt quite a bit since I was apparently considered useless as an active participant in the proceedings. I feared that my pan might get hopelessly burned by this rather happy-go-lucky crew of attendants during the boiling process. Also, I have found that it is easy to lend something, but the difficulties in retrieving it can be unbelievable. My initial enthusiasm suffered a fast burn out.

A little later that same winter when the snowdrifts still showed no signs of subsiding, another farmer acquaintance informed me in an avuncular manner that he thought he might take my syrup pan and "just make myself a little syrup back in the woods." "Indeed!" I thought. It gave me a really lonesome feeling thinking of my little pan back in this man's woods. For he did not have your typical cozy type of woodlot. His woods were cut up by steep, walled gorges where you could peer down hundreds of feet to observe little rippling streams of water far below. The acreage of his woods was so vast and so wild that I am sure some animals live there that are generally considered extinct. Perhaps *eohippus*, the horse of pre-history who was about the size of a fox, had toes instead of hooves, and was ancestor to our present-day horse!

The scenery was breathtaking and beautiful, but I did not think it was domesticated enough for my syrup pan, which I treasured as much as any of the other family heirlooms. In as gracious a manner as possible, I managed to convey the impression to this man that he might be wise to look elsewhere for his sugaring accessories.

Although I turned down these two business opportunities, I did begin to wonder why I couldn't make syrup by myself. I borrowed an immensely helpful book called *The Backyard Sugar Maker* from the library. I hunted around the farmstead and rounded up sap pails, spiles, an auger, a syrup skimmer and a few other necessary supplies. Then I began the really hard part of building a satisfactory outdoor fireplace for my boiling operations. I finally constructed a fully enclosed fireplace with a sliding door in front for feeding in wood, and a piece of stovepipe with a damper in it to carry smoke away from the syrup pan.

Then I began my years as a syrup-maker, and developed quite a business making and selling maple cream, maple fudge, fancy maple cakes in the shape of leaves, log cabins, Indian chiefs, and stars. I also stirred maple sugar, which is a dry granular sugar greatly cherished by those early sugarmakers, the Indians.

I probably never would have got started in this delightful, exacting business if I had not listened as these two neighborly persons attempted deftly to separate me from the coveted syrup pan, attempts that I cannily circumvented by keeping it in steady use myself!

My soul waiteth for the Lord more than they that watch for the morning.

Psalm 130:5

Knocking On The Door

During April I was watching my calendar closely, for I was busy calculating just when would be the best time to view the bloodroot in some distant woods. It is the only wood around here where I have found this lovely pure white flower that belongs to the poppy family. I had not been able to visit these woods for quite a few years. Along in mid-April my Stonehengian-type calculations finally indicated that now was the best time to find the bloodroot in flower.

Early one morning my dog Lira and I set out. The day was breezy and sunny, still with a distinct snow chill in the air. We safely traversed some immense stubbly cornfields, negotiated the creek at a fairly shallow place where the water spreads out over a shoal of gravel, and then headed off through a swampy, brushy area. Little flames of scarlet flowers were running along the branches of the swamp maples and we flushed up a woodcock who strongly favors this kind of damp, soggy land. We passed over some hemlock knolls with huge fallen logs where the partridge sometimes begin drumming in early February, especially on mild days. Eventually we came to higher ground where there is an extensive woods of maple, butternut, beech and ash, still leafless, allowing the sunshine to penetrate to the woods' floor for the benefit of the early spring flowers.

There was a lovely waiting hush in the woods, as if some great conductor's baton was raised and would come sweeping down at any moment to start the first movement of a great symphony of spring. The only noise was the brisk knocking of a woodpecker, pounding at the door of a new and longed-for season.

There on a gentle southern slope were the bloodroot flowers as I remembered them, great patches of pure white, golden-centered blossoms, each one held in the protective clasp of a lovely, pale green, celery-colored leaf. After admiring the bloodroot for awhile I tramped around the woods a bit and found the brick and stone outlines of a vanished structure. Possibly it is a Celtic ruin of pre-Columbian antiquity, such as have been found in New Hampshire and are the subject of heated archaeological debates. Probably the remains are not really that old; I have never been able to decide just what they were.

A long narrow area, partially dug into a hillside is walled with old bricks and flat fieldstones, and is about five yards long and a yard and a half across. These dimensions do not seem right for any woods activity that I can think of, such as operating a still, a maple sugar arch, the burning of charcoal, a potashery and so on. The only idea that seems even marginally possible is that it was a place to dry apples. Perhaps the walls were roofed over with flat stones and apple slices laid on them to dry by a slow fire underneath.

There is quite an orchard of more or less wild apples close at hand which perhaps was once a farm orchard. In fact, propped up against a nearby apple tree is a lovely old hand-crafted ladder. This is a very delicate ladder, light and easy to carry, and still bearing traces of old-fashioned red paint. It is a fruit ladder, used to pick cherries and pears and apples.

Jacob's biblical experience seems to indicate that angels are partial to ladders. If I went to sleep in this wistful, awakening April woods, perhaps I would see them using

32

this finely crafted ladder, made long ago in some farm workshop, perhaps climbing up to heaven, or just up into the trees to see if the apple blossoms will be ready to open soon.

Thou sendest forth thy Spirit...Thou renewest the face of the earth.

Psalm 104:30

The Pond

There is a little pond down my road that may not seem like much if someone has just come from viewing Lake Placid, or Lake Memphremagogg, or the Lake of the Woods in Canada. But it is a beloved landmark for me. It is a short and easy distance in case my time is limited and I cannot go on a longer walk, or if the weather is threatening. I always see something new and interesting or beautiful there, or perhaps just instructive.

It is a modest-sized pond fed by springs seeping down from the Folded Hills. The water collects in a hollow that perhaps was scooped out by the last glacier. In wet weather the overflow goes into a drainage pipe beneath the old road and on down to the main stream. In dry weather the pond used to sometimes dry up completely, forcing more than one muskrat family to make the dangerous overland journey to the main creek. But a few years ago my woodsman friend who actually holds title to

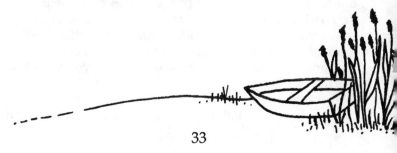

the pond hired a backhoe operator to dig it out, removing a great amount of silt and debris and substantially deepening the pond, so now it may get low but never dries up.

Through most of the summer I see a solitary great blue heron standing there, studying the water with a fishy looking eye, but now in April I startle up a pair who take to the air in clumsy, labored flight. Springtime is no time to be alone and the pond is a honeymoon place for the herons and also for the wild mallard ducks who spend a few days on its quiet waters before building a nest along the edge of the main creek. Painted turtles bask on logs along the edge, chorus frogs call from it in the early spring, and the quiet waters form a perfect mirror for the green of the nearby pines or the pumpkin gold and scarlet of the maples in autumn.

After my neighbor had the pond dug out he stocked it with rock bass and blue gill. He placed several small wooden rafts in the pond to provide shade for the fish, and occasionally dumped some fish food into the water. However, an amazing and unaccountable piscatorial transaction must have taken place, for several years after the fish stocking program he decided that his fish would be well established and that it would be a nice time to do a little fishing. But all he got were two or three very muddy looking bullheads.

"Bullheads!" he snorted, eyeing me suspiciously as if he suspected that I might somehow be responsible. "How did those get there?" "Well, I don't really know," I replied, adding defensively, "But I think bullheads are delicious. You fry them with a little piece of bacon, and have a mess of cowslip greens to go with them, and a bit of freshly grated horseradish. . .Then you've really got something." "Hmph," he said, not deeming this culinary information worthy of a reply.

My friend's long-range plan for the pond was as a fishin' hole for his grandchildren. Off and on, he has muttered about the "trash fish." Eventually he gave up the idea of stocking the pond with pan fish and just planted some young maple trees on the banks so that some day it would make a cool, shady spot for picnics.

As the seasons slowly change, so the pond changes too, always different and yet always, the same, and I recall the lovely words from Isaiah:

I will make the wilderness a pool of water and the dry land springs of water.

Isaiah 41:18

Garden's Up

March in Upstate New York is often cold and blustery but, even so, many of us begin to think of planting a garden. Several years ago, a correspondent who supplied news from her village to our local weekly newspaper wrote for the March 9th issue: "This week it looks like spring! Several people have said it's supposed to turn nasty again tomorrow, but I'm just going to enjoy it while it's here. And buy some peas for planting in three weeks."

She was a busy young woman with a family, her newspaper work, and course work at a nearby community college. Her items were always well written, often humorous, and contained a good deal of material of interest to her readership. Peas are always of interest, especially in March when some days are likely to be so warm and springlike that it can be difficult to hold back from planting the garden on the spot. An elderly neighbor of mine, usually a reliable guru on all rural matters, did indeed do this one year in March when some especially beguiling days ruined his good judgment. Subsequent blizzards and hard freezes spoiled it all, and he had to replant everything, including the peas.

35

The correspondent's column suddenly ended in early summer when she became ill with cancer. After only two months she died. I remembered what she had written a few months before about buying seeds for her garden, and I wondered, if she had known her life was almost over, would she still have made a garden and planted peas, or would she have wanted to do other things.

I have had a lovely lifetime of growing peas and other "garden stuff," as country people often refer to their vegetables. When I was a small child our garden was plowed and cultivated by a team of large workhorses. They were dear, familiar horses and when the season was advanced far enough so that the rows of delicate new greenery needed cultivating, they did this task. They took the corners, however, with an insouciant ease that always brought my mother out on the run to convey urgent messages to my father, such as, "Those horses are stepping on (tearing up) the peas (carrots) (swiss chard) (corn)," and so forth. My father had his hands full trying to steer two vast plowhorses with huge feet through the rows of tender vegetables and at the same time attempting to calm my mother's alarm. With the modern day, easily maneuverable, tillers, gardening isn't nearly so exciting!

Later on, when the garden was far enough along for weeding and hoeing, I followed my father like a little shadow waiting for him to hand me a tender new carrot or a handful of bright green pea pods just beginning to swell with the tiny sweet flavored juicy peas.

When I grew up and had my own garden I always planted peas in early May when the ground was beginning to warm up. (Never mind all of those Good Friday die-hard pea planters who were out much earlier trying to plant peas in a snowstorm!) For a few years I always planted Little Marvel peas, and later on I tried Laxton's peas, but I finally settled on Lincoln peas as best suited to my garden soil. Even though others have ever pressed onward to new pea experiences such as Alaska peas (extra-early), Wando (will produce even in hot weather, it is claimed), or Green-Arrow peas (they "resist cold weather"), I have faithfully stayed with my Lincolns. They are always tender and sweet, the pods fill up uniformly, and it is a pleasure to sit down on the woodshed steps and shell out a panful for lunch or for freezing. I love everything about peas, the pewter bluish-green leaves, the small twining tendrils, and the pure white blossoms that look like little dainty ribbon hairbows.

The rows of peas in my garden taught me quite a few things. I learned that about two thorough hoeings and weedings are enough. Sometimes it is possible to stir up a garden too much. For peas are shallow-rooted and it is best not to disturb the roots unduly. Also, peas love plenty of moisture and a cool earth so I leave a few weeds here and there to provide shade and support for the plants to lean against. You always have to watch peas closely. If you look the other way for just a moment you might miss those flat green pods when they are full of tender, delicious green peas just right for cooking. I can make an entire meal just from a big bowl of peas with a little butter, pepper and salt. That's right—no new potatoes, no cream sauce—just new peas. Many of my acquaintances tell me reproachfully that they always cook new peas and new potatoes together in a milk or cream sauce and didn't I ever try it? I just say that I am never able to get that many ingredients ready at the same time. After all, I am the one who hastily returned the book, *The Frugal Gourmet Cooks American* to the library when I discovered a recipe in it that called for 25 ingredients. My cooking style is simpler!

One summer when I was between jobs and with not very good prospects for another, I planted a very large tilled area with peas. I had no market for them and thought perhaps I would not be able to sell so many. But I found a busy roadside market that would take all that I could supply them with. So when the peas were ready to be moved, I arose every morning just when it was getting light enough so that one could grope around with some degree of accuracy in the pea patch. I picked washtubs full and bushel baskets full of the peas while the day was still cool and liveable. New little cottontail rabbits played in the meadow grasses and the wood thrushes were practicing their flutelike contralto notes. Then I drove to the roadside stand and as I unloaded the peas, early customers would exclaim "Peas! They've just been picked! They're really fresh. Oh! I love new garden peas!" And the peas quickly sold out and I had a good summer even though it hadn't seemed too promising at the beginning.

Another well-remembered pea year involved a neighbor's pea patch. A young farm wife and her husband drilled in an acre or so of peas at one end of an oat field. When they were ready to be picked, she simply told all of her friends and neighbors to come and help themselves, free of charge. At first no one could believe that the peas were really free—there must be a catch somewhere—so everyone held back a bit. But soon we were all out there with pails, kettles and baskets, the sunshine hot on our backs, the killdeer calling from a nearby meadow. We picked and talked and laughed with neighbors we had hardly known before. Two farm women who had been barely speaking, due to a line fence dispute, forgot all about the fences and found they had all sorts of things in common, including a love for quilting. As I finished filling my pails, destined for a neighbor house-bound with arthritis, I heard the two ladies planning an afternoon's quilting session together. All sorts of nice, unexpected things can happen in a pea patch!

I think if I knew I was going to leave this lovely green flowering earth in August, the peas would still be planted. In times of turmoil and difficulties, I have always found comfort in the garden. I cannot think that I would feel distress or fear if Jesus came to me in the garden and said,

"Follow me."

As one whom his mother comforts, so I will comfort you.
Isaiah 66:13

Red Birds

Some years ago I worked at a home and school for handicapped children near the Blue Ridge Mountains in Virginia. When the lovely early Virginia spring came, I admired the dogwood flowers, the saucer magnolias, the delicate redbud blossoms, the pink azaleas and other species that I had known before only in books. There were also birds new to me. One day, in the soft, timeless air of a Virginia spring I saw a little red bird darting about among the cinnamon vines that shaded a porch on the east side of the home.

I had never seen this bird before and did not have my bird guides with me, so I asked another housemother what kind of a bird that little red bird was. I pointed it out to her as it inspected the vines, apparently looking for a nice nesting place. "Red bird?" she repeated uncertainly in the delightful southern accent that melodiously fractures many words enunciated so crisply in the north. Looking at me in helpless bewilderment she said, "Why it's a-a-a redbird," and sighed. After dispensing this confusing bit of information, she drifted off on the endless rounds of bed-making, cleaning, childcare and laundry that kept us busy.

When I was home again, securely surrounded by my bird books, I decided that the redbird I had seen in Virginia was the summer tanager. The male is an all-over rosy red, while the female and young are an orange-yellow. This redbird winters in Central and South America. In the springtime, after the exhausting northward flight across the Gulf of Mexico, parks and gardens of coastal cities are often filled with a "rain of redbirds."

However, "redbird" can be quite another sort to someone from a different background. A correspondent from Illinois writes "Red birds are nesting in the crepe-myrtle bush by the house. Their lovely whistle 'whe-at ye-ar,' with variations, truly is the Song of Spring." And I knew that her redbirds are cardinals, for his is what they say.

Here in the north an old-timer friend who finds God while trout fishing, refers to the scarlet tanager, lover of the damp, streamside woods, as redbird. He said he didn't think he'd ever seen a prettier bird, with its flame-like feathers and coal-black wings.

As my search for the real redbird goes on, I find ever more, even including the tiny rufous hummingbird of the far west. I have concluded that a redbird is ...well...it's a redbird.

At the moment my own cherished redbird (cardinal) is up in the grapevines that scramble over the lilac bushes outside my south window. The grapevines probably should have been rooted out several springs ago but it "got away from me." Perhaps it is just as well because several cardinals are spending a great deal of time there feeding on the clusters of frosty wild grapes. Most of the grape leaves have fallen and the few that are left are a pale, transparent yellow, as fragile as old lace. The chilly autumn sunshine filters through them like light slanting through a bit of stained glass.

It is nice to see the cardinals on these rather dull, dark November days, and now that they are here they will stay on for the sunflower seeds at my birdfeeding station, which I put into operation when the first heavy snowfall comes. You can indulge in quite a bit of oneupsmanship around here if you have a dependable supply of cardinals at your feeders!

Redbird seems to be a tender, loving appellation, without any special taxonomic pretensions, that we give to the

40

red bird closest to our own heart.

And out of the ground the Lord God formed every beast of the field, and every fowl of the air; and brought them unto Adam to see what he would call them: and whatsoever Adam called every living creature, that was the name thereof.

Genesis 2:19

Trash and Treasure

By late May, the bleeding heart is in full bloom, the lovely rosy red hearts suspended at regular intervals along the gracefully arching horizontal stems. The daylight hours override the darkness now and even at 8:15 p.m. dusk has hardly begun to make advances. As I sit in my dooryard a hummingbird comes to the bleeding heart. This is a female with quiet shades of green and grayish and a bit of white on the tip of the tail. The tiny bird needs to hover directly beneath the flowers, pointing its bill straight up into the blossoms' nectary, at the same time taking care not to hit the ground. But it seems to be no problem. The busy wings hum. Sometimes the bird hovers in a circling movement beneath the flowers as if held by a fine thread, the backwash from its wings ruffling the tender green foliage like a miniature whirlwind.

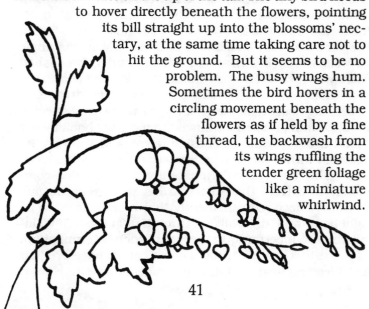

It is an exquisite, joyful time as I watch the little bird, who transacts so much business with the flowers, "do" every blossom, one by one. I think back to the day last summer when I rescued the source of this enchantment from my bookdealer friend who is a good but somewhat erratic gardener. Early in the spring he had dug out and thrown away the perennial bleeding heart that had been growing in a flowerbed by his front porch. "You threw out bleeding heart!" I said in despair, for I had long wished that I possessed some of this lovely plant. "Dug it right out, and threw it away," he announced. "I wanted it right out of there." I realized sadly that there is no accounting for taste. I even knew someone once who didn't like hollyhocks. There was no chance of retrieving the bleeding heart for it had long since been carried away by the trash men. So I merely sighed and thought wistfully of the first time I had ever seen bleeding heart. It was in a little shaded nook by the modest home in the Township of Worth that housed a widely patronized second-hand shop. Inside the building there were all sorts of useful artifacts as well as a few really nice antiques, all quite inexpensive for those days of the '50s and '60s. Most of the yard was sun-baked and barren. But in the angle between the old brown shingled house and the woodshed there was a vast flowering mound of bleeding heart that more than made up for deficiencies in the landscape.

Bleeding heart remained a lovely memory until one day in late summer when I chanced to meet my book dealer friend again. While discussing lawns and gardens, he declared with some exasperation that the bleeding heart was viable once more. Apparently he had failed completely to extract the tubers in his springtime digging work. He declared vehemently that he was going to go right home and "dig it all out, throw it right away." "Well," I ventured, uncertainly in the face of such determination, "If you're just going to throw it away, could I have it? I just love bleeding heart." "Oh sure, you can have it. Have it all," he promised generously. I just happened to have a handy cardboard carton in my car, so I stopped by his house and picked up the battle-scarred bleeding heart, a chunky bit of root with a little foliage feebly trying to make contact with the sunshine and fresh air. Mid-August is probably not the best time to transplant things, but I put it in some good deep dirt by the little stone-paved pathway to my cabin. I watered it frequently and in early winter covered it with a thick mulch of peat moss. And now here it is, my lovely treasure, unwanted and treated quite inconsiderately for a time, bringing joy and comfort to a little fast-winged hummingbird, and peace and beauty to my yard.

Surely you have read this scripture? "The stone which the builders rejected as worthless turned out to be the most important of all. This was done by the Lord; what a wonderful sight it is!"

Mark 12:10-11

The Teacher Bird

By the end of May, the petal moon of late spring was waxing strongly. I began to find glossy yellow buttercups, a reminder that the season was moving right along. And that it was time to go to the woods across the creek in search of starflower.

These woods are, for the most part, low and wet, producing an abundance of blue beech, red maple, the northern wild raisin, leatherwood, poison ivy and marsh marigolds. But there are hemlock knolls throughout the woods, carpeted with fragrant brown needles and supporting such plants as ground pine, wild ginger, hepaticas, and the Indian cucumber-root. And last summer I

43

had discovered starflower's stiff little circlet of leaves, but the flowers which I had never seen were already gone.

So now, on the 30th of May, after almost a year of anticipation, I waded through the creek, climbed a steep bank on my hands and knees, and then followed an old wagon road into the heart of the deep woods. There I located a drift of these little, pure white, six-or seven-pointed flowers, blooming with an astral purity in the dimness beneath the hemlocks.

Along the old road I flushed up a little brown bird who was apparently suffering from some traumatic ailment, for she fluttered her wings and dragged her tail and altogether seemed the worse for wear. But she took the trouble to go slowly enough so that I could follow her, and looked back over her shoulder occasionally to check my progress.

For a moment or two, I will have to admit that I was so confused that I decided this bird was a bobwhite. This was an astounding bit of bird identification, and I still can offer no sensible excuse for it, especially for a graduate of Cornell's Ornithology 101! My second guess was a wood thrush, but then I realized that although her white breast had sepia-black markings and her back was a soft leaf brown, it was a smaller bird. But as she flopped about on the ground and hobbled weakly up to perch for a moment on a protruding root by the side of a gully, I finally saw the orange-crowned head with the dark stripes and knew that here was the ovenbird or golden-crowned thrush, known to me before only by its insistent, disembodied call of "tea-cher, tea-cher, tea-cher" somewhere in the filtered gloom of the hemlocks. This little pronouncement builds up in volume until at the end it is so emphatic that all the vireos, the veeries, the thrushes and the other warblers (the ovenbird is really a warbler) lapse into a stunned silence. It is hard to see how such a big voice can come from such a small bird.

I knew the bird was anxious to draw me away from the

nest, and I did not want to worry her unnecessarily, so before I followed her I took only a quick look in the spot where she had made her entrance. There, skillfully inserted among the shining leaves of the Canada mayflowers was her rounded nest, in the shape of a dutch oven, with an opening toward the woods' track. I stooped down but could not really see inside, and I did not touch anything. Too close attention to a nest can cause the birds to abandon it, or can serve as a signal to predators that there is something of interest that should be investigated. So I merely stayed long enough to note the location of the nest in relation to a hemlock tree where a pileated woodpecker had made a series of oblong excavations while searching for carpenter ants.

Then I obligingly followed the little mother for about a quarter of a mile through the woods. When she felt satisfied that I was at a suitable distance from the nest, she smugly deserted me, finding her way back circuitously through the woods to the treasure where her heart had been all the time. Leaving me to flounder back to the woods' road as best I could.

Late in August I returned to the now empty ovenbird nest. I found that the ovenbird is a connoisseur of the finest nesting materials available in the wild. The nest was composed of tiny hemlock twigs, bits of leaves and leaf stems, porcupine quills, the long, coarse porcupine guard hairs, and even the soft gray underfur. The winter hair of the deer, shed in the spring, had also been used. There were the gleaming dark wiry stems of maidenhair fern, and in the inner nest lining there was much soft reddish brown fur that had been plucked from the unrolling fiddleheads of ferns. Altogether a most satisfactorily built nest for the small bird who so persistently calls for "tea-cher" in the heart of the remote hemlock woods.

All day long I praise you and proclaim your glory.
                                                    Psalm 71:8

Making a Garden

For quite some time after we moved to our lakeside farm near Henderson, our road was a typical dirt road with seasonal mud holes, some bone jarring bumps, and immense dust clouds in dry weather. Besides providing access to farms and lakeshore cottages, the road eventually ended at an Army rifle range at the end of Stony Point. Truckloads of soldiers were taken there from barracks at Sackets Harbor to practice shooting out over the lake.

Either during the Second World War or just before, the Army decided to upgrade this road to a smooth concrete highway. The contract was given to a Watertown construction firm owned by an Italian who mostly employed Italian workers. There was a great deal of machinery and workmen involved and, since transportation was not as simple then as it is now, the contractor approached my father about renting a house across from our farm. He hoped to house some of his workers there and also a watchman to keep an eye on the expensive road machinery. The house was a little drafty for winter living but in the summertime when these men would be there it was cool and pleasant. The house was part of a woodsy farm my father rented to run young stock through the summer months. Mother and Father put in some basic furniture, and with quite a bit of trepidation rented the house to the Italian road company. But they need not have worried. The men who stayed there were all nice, quiet men, closely attached to their families in Watertown, and there were no wild goings-on. The one who stayed there the most was an elderly man who was really a gardener at heart, a fine example of the rural peasantry who had always lived close to the land in Italy.

There was no drinking water at the rental house so he came to our well for water and bought milk, eggs, and sometimes a little meat from us for simple meals he

46

prepared on a small oil stove. We became good friends with this gentle, kindly man and were somewhat concerned when he mentioned a few times that he was putting in a "little garden" just back of the house. We did not see how he could get anything to grow in the wind-blown, hot and arid bit of thin, stony soil and were afraid he was letting himself in for a big disappointment. But we didn't want to interfere so we just sighed and looked at each other when he mentioned his garden.

One mid-summer evening when the fireflies were beginning to light up the gathering dusk, our friend asked us to come over and sit awhile and see his garden. We all walked over, sure it would be a sad looking affair, and trying to think of consoling remarks to make. But we were in for quite a surprise. As we sat on the back porch and our friend lighted his pipe in the peaceful silence, we saw a beautiful small garden—velvety green tomato plants tied to stakes with carefully torn strips of old rags, and burdened with big, heavy, sun-ripened tomatoes; lettuces as green and fresh as if the morning dew was still on them; tender green beans, thick green peppers, onions, and even a row of golden carrots. We did not see even one weed, a state of affairs quite astonishing to us, accustomed as we were to some thrifty weeds in our own garden.

We were just about speechless so we quietly sat and admired this lovely miracle that had changed a little piece of wasteland into a productive, beautiful garden plot. We never did really find out our host's gardening secrets, although between sessions of filling his pipe and puffing out fragrant clouds of smoke he said that he watered the plants quite often from the rain barrel at the back door. Also he had found a pile of very ancient composted manure by the fallen-in barn and he had worked pails full of this into the soil before planting time. Then, too, he had spent all of the long evening hours out there with his garden, close at hand for whatever needed to be done.

As we left we told him what a wonderful garden he had and he said shyly that it gave him something to do after the day's road work was over. I think his real secret was that he "lived" in the garden, creating a little haven of love, peace and security in his transient life.

But some seeds fell in good soil, and the plants bore grain; some had one hundred grains, others sixty and others thirty.

Matthew 13:8

Under the Pines

A few years ago almost everyone was out digging in farm dumps, wherever they could be found, searching for old bottles and any other ancient detritus that might be around. Colored electrical insulators also ranked high in collecting circles at the time. Eventually I, too, was seized with this digging fever and seldom took a walk without at least a trowel and a basket for use in carrying home my finds. Since I was so familiar with the surrounding countryside, I knew where more than one old cellarhole and nearby dump were located, perhaps on the edge of some leafy woods' glade or along some road so obliterated and obscure that it is known to hardly any present day inhabitants.

In general, the dumps attached to those forgotten dwellings were never very large because our ancestors had a natural recycling society. Everything was used until it was worn out and even that was not always the end of it. Rags were woven into carpets, or sold to the traveling ragman and eventually used in making paper. Bits of broken dishes became cherished accouterments for little girls' dollhouses, scrap iron was sold to the scrap ironman and so on.

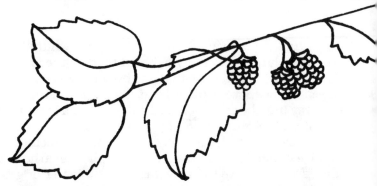

I did find a few nice things in the leafy digs where I made my rounds as the seasons came and went. Spring was a good time to do a little spadework, for the frost always heaved a few artifacts to the surface in the same way that it always produces a new crop of stones here in the northeast for the farmer to pick off his meadows. I found an old cowbell that struck a beautiful mellow note, a graniteware kettle even with a cover, and a little square ironstone butter pat that I still treasure. But mostly I found bottles, some quite old but probably not very valuable, and quite often broken.

There was one huge old dump on the edge of an adjoining woods that I longed to explore but I only looked at it with covetous eyes if I happened to be in those woods. Wild red raspberries grew thick and heavy around a fallen-down sugar shanty near the dump so I usually did some berry picking there in July. But I did not disturb the dump, for it belonged to my elderly neighbor who was such a good resource person for my country-type problems that arose with monotonous regularity. I had heard him give some alarming forecasts of what would happen if any of "those blasted diggers" got into his dump. He said he was going to excavate it himself some day. His dump spanned a time from the arrival of the first settler on his farm right down to his own occupancy, so it was hard to keep my hands off it, but I did. I was careful not to let him know that, in a small way, I too was one of "those blasted diggers."

Eventually, however, I found a dig of my own that was also quite large. Down my old road there is the foundation of a large farmhouse that has been gone about 60 or 70 years now. Several times I had climbed down the stone stairway into the cellarhole and poked around looking for any bits of ancient memorabilia which might be around. They proved to be remarkably scarce, but I remembered that there had been an earlier and smaller cellarhole on this farm where the first settler had built the original small dwelling house. It was pleasantly located near an everflowing spring of cool, clear water and was shaded by apple trees. It occurred to me that perhaps the later family members who had built the larger house had used the smaller foundation as a dump. And so one day I took a spade down into this venerable cellarhole to see if there might be some priceless treasures underneath the thick layers of humus and leaves that had accumulated here.

Over the next few weeks I spent quite a few interesting hours in this quiet, shady spot, on the former site of a once bustling family farm, now frequented only by whitetail deer who blew and snorted and leaped gracefully away when I appeared, and other forest folk who drank from the spring and enjoyed the wild fruits that grew there. Lira would go to sleep in some comfortable spot and I would dig away, mentally mapping out my excavations almost as carefully as an archaeologist who might be working on the ruins of some lost city of the Incas or other scholarly project. I carefully deposited each spadeful of dirt and stones and leaves some little distance away where it would not cover more deeply some prospective digging area. And I did find some very interesting remnants of earlier days—chips from earthenware jars and jugs, cracked pieces from lovely old flowered dinnerware, shards of flow-blue dishes, and splintered pieces of glass from old frosted, beaded water glasses. My bits and pieces were lovely, but everything was broken. Finally, late one afternoon when the wood thrushes were beginning to tune up their flutelike notes for an evening concert, the realization came to me that, interesting as this heap was, it was unlikely that a whole piece of anything was going to be found in it. No one was going to throw away good dishes or handy kitchen utensils. There were not even any bottles, as the people who had lived there had apparently not been consumers of the patent medicines or "bitters" (a liquor containing bitter herbs, roots and usually alcohol for medical purposes), so common in those days. I carefully spread the heaps of dirt and leaves back over the bottom of the cellarhole and smoothed everything over so that my raccoon and opossum friends would not fall into any of my excavations. And I gave up my pastime as a dump digger.

Not long after, I was walking through a plantation of pines that had been planted on the same farm and almost stepped on the neck of a bottle poking up through the thick carpet of pine needles. I gently pulled and tugged on the bottle, expecting at any moment to find I was just holding a broken piece in my hand. But my efforts yielded an exquisite bottle with no crack or flaw of any kind to mar the infinitely pale blue coloring. Tiny, delicate bubbles were trapped forever in the old glass. One side of the rather high, rectangular bottle was plain. The other side was lettered as follows:

C.I. Hood & Co.
HOOD'S
SARSA
PARILLA
LOWELL, MASS.
68

I loved the way the makers had left out a bothersome hyphen in the word "Sarsaparilla." And I wondered about Lowell, Mass., which I had always thought of as a famous New England mill town. Subsequent investigation revealed

51

that it was also the sarsaparilla capital of the world. Most of all I pondered the problem of why the bottle was heaved away in this particular place, which must have been a cow or sheep pasture on the old farm. Who knows? As the Swiss journalist Henri Amiel suggested, it is good to leave a little place for mystery in our hearts.

The Battle of the Stub

This year the first blow in the annual Battle of the Stub was struck on May 7th. The battles of Thermopylae, Waterloo and Armageddon may be more highly publicized, but none could be fought with such fervor as this ongoing fracas.

The stub is the hollow remnant of a maple tree that stands in the hedgerow near my cabin. The top was lost in some long-forgotten storm. To a mere human it seems quite decrepit and of little value. It even seems likely to topple over in some gale. But it is esteemed in the tribal memories handed down by inhabitants who knew the tree as a strong and leafy fortress providing security and good, healthful, maple seeds, a dietary item highly regarded by many birds and animals. Back then, no one would have believed that one day the great tree would be just a weather-scarred bit of wood, with not a single green leaf.

But beauty is in the eye of the beholder and the stub is loved by all sorts of wild folk. This morning, the beginning of a fragrant, growing day in early May, I see that the bedding of a deer mouse, one of the most recent small stub persons, has been thrown out and is lying in a mud puddle.

Deer mouse is a real connoisseur of nice bedding materials. I study with regret the nest of carefully selected silvery thistledown, soft, frayed cedar fencepost bark, tiny slivers of punky wood, and the very softest tips of new moss that the mouse could find. Some other would-be tenant has piratically tossed all this out through one of the woodpecker holes that perforate the stub.

One summer a pair of flickers and a pair of starlings spent the entire season squabbling over possession of the nesting site. The flickers tossed out the nesting material of the starlings, only to see the starlings return with even more supplies, including a bit of greenery. Starlings always like to have a leafy twig or a piece from a fresh, growing plant in their nest. Flickers do not have any special nesting material. The female just lays her glossy white eggs on chips at the bottom of the cavity. So the starlings probably simply tucked their bits of material in on top of the chips, to have it promptly seized and thrown out the nearest window. I do not think either pair hatched any eggs that summer.

Regardless of the turmoil in the upper stories of the stub, there is always a resident chipmunk with a burrow deep down among the roots. Chipmunk often sits atop the stub like a small, toast-golden Buddha, engrossed in the surrounding scene. I imagine this is a hereditary home that goes to chipmunk heirs, entailed as estates were passed on in England.

The location is desirable because it is surrounded by many of the wild pasture gooseberry bushes, much esteemed by chipmunk. I, too, hold them in high regard. When they ripen, chipmunk picks them and sits on a cool rock, gravely shucking off the prickly outer skin and feeding on the delicious mild fruits. I like to make a rosy-pink jelly out of the same fruits, but this longing is seldom fulfilled, for chipmunk almost always gets there first and I come in a poor second. Indeed chipmunks everywhere seem to go on a gooseberry alert when the wild fruits are ripening.

Only once was I able to gather enough for a good batch

53

of jelly. I do not really mind my regular defeat in this battle of wits, and I hope that the stub folk have a happy and fairly peaceful summer. Mary Tudor said, "When I am dead and opened you shall find Calais lying in my heart." I am convinced that engraved on the hearts of many of the little wild folk are two words—"The Stub".

Do not store up riches for yourselves here on earth, where moths and rust destroy, and robbers break in and steal. Instead, store up riches for yourself in heaven, where moths and rust cannot destroy, and robbers cannot break in and steal. For your heart will always be where your riches are.

Matthew 6:19-21

The Chokecherry Tree

These days the entire earth is in trouble. We cannot help wondering if our efforts to save our planet, small as they sometimes must be, can really make a difference. But we have to start somewhere.

Now in midsummer I look at a chokecherry, a native small shrubby tree, that grows in my yard. Already it is loaded with small fruits ripening to a dusky red, with the flavor of cherry wine. I hardly ever see a fully ripe chokecherry, for all of the wild folk are well disposed toward these fruits. They waste no time as they hasten to check out this well provisioned feeding station.

Several years ago I found this tree lying on the ground, uprooted and tossed aside by a bulldozer in a road improvement project. At first I left it there. After all, chokecherries are so common. Aren't they? But even while considering the matter I found myself digging a hole in my yard—a large one, for the tree was tall and leafy, at least for a chokecherry, which often is only a shrub. After re-planting the tree, many pails of water were needed to ease the transition to a new location. Now I am glad that I was able to save the little "tree of life." The clusters of foamy white flowers are lovely in the springtime. And so are the fledgling catbirds who are in its leafy branches on this sunny day, learning the difference between ripe and not ripe.

Picking Blackcaps

The blackcaps are thick and lush this year and I find nice ones in almost every thicket and fencerow. One evening when a stifling July day is beginning to cool down a bit I even see gentle cottontail rabbit muzzling off some of the sweet delicious fruits near the cabin. She is not disturbed by any of the Bittersweet Garden folk, for Lira is sound asleep under a snowball bush and Altoona is on the roof where she likes to go sometimes to do her serious thinking.

I have had a dish of blackcaps for supper, combined with a few red raspberries and a handful of gleaming red currants. I remember a friend saying gloomily, "Well, all you can do with currants is make them into jelly," She seemed to be amazed at the notion of eating them fresh. But combined with some berries they make a summery country dessert, cool and agreeable on sultry days.

The blackcaps are harder to find some years and also their location usually varies from year to year. Two years ago I found a modest amount of berries. It had been a hot, tiring afternoon and I had managed to get mixed up with some stinging nettles, which are most unfriendly plants. (Yes, I know nettles make a great nettles soup, and make a valuable addition to the compost pile.) I made jam from some of the berries and gave one small jar to a usually taciturn neighbor. She admitted that the jam was good. Since then she has often said, "Do you remember that little jar of blackcap jam you gave me? I really liked that." And she would add hopefully, "I think maybe blackcap is my favorite jam. Where do you find your blackcaps?" I answer vaguely "Well, you just have to get out and look around. Walk along the meadow fencerows and the edge of the woods, and in the upland pastures. You just never know where you will find really nice ones. But some years they are mostly seedy and dried up." My neighbor never looks convinced at this review of the blackcap situation. She probably thinks it is entirely within my power to lead her directly to Elysian fields of the berries. It does not help when I add whimsically, I think they just pick up their little roots and move to other places sometimes. They love to settle down near a bit of old rail fence."

This summer when the berries are plentiful I will make up some jam, medium sized jars this time, to give at Christmas. Even the hard to please folk who "have everything" might welcome a taste of summertime when the temperature is sinking and fingers of drifting snow are closing in the roads. Some gifts have to be planned a long time ahead!

Never Seen a Wild Bear

Several years ago I heard of a bear incident involving a couple who live in the country not too far away. The wife, an early riser, was up about 6 a.m. She looked out a window and saw a young black bear come into the yard. She was entranced and watched for some time as it ambled around the premises and finally plunged off into a nearby woodland. Later on, when her husband was awake, she told him about the early morning visitor and was full of remorse when he said, "You actually saw a real wild black bear? And didn't wake me? Why didn't you get me up? I've never *seen* a real wild black bear!"

This made quite an impression on me for it reflected so well my own experience with wild black bears (or any other kind, for that matter)—absolutely none. I, too, thought, with just a touch of apprehension, it would be wonderful to see a native bear. What would my dog Lira do, and what would the bear do? Our black bears are not considered dangerous unless they have cubs or their habitat is invaded too deeply by camps, resorts, shopping malls and so on.

In recent years I had seen signs of the presence of black bears—a patch of Indian turnip (jack-in-the-pulpit) sort of blasted out of the ground, the bulbs torn off and missing. The bear is about the only one of the wild folk that eats these bulbs, for they contain a fiery juice that affects most tongues like a mixture of sulphuric acid and powdered glass. I had also seen several rotted logs torn apart in such an ambitious way that it probably was done by a bear looking for the juicy grubs he strongly favors as good gourmet woods' food. And a hornet's nest, down in some tangled weeds, had been torn apart, leaving only one or two desolate survivors crawling feebly around, and an extensive area of squashed vegetation.

So it went until late July when I went berrying in a woods just beyond the hillside pasture. Under an immense maple tree in this pasture there is a spring and both Lira and I began picking red raspberries, gradually moving into the woods. This woods had been lumbered off fairly recently in a hit-or-miss fashion, and the berries grew thick and lush in many of the openings left by this calamitous operation.

The raspberries were dead ripe and ready at a touch to drop off into my kettle. They glowed like jewels against the green of the leaves, and in no time my container was filled.

Some wild berry pickers had also been indulging in the berries. A tuft of golden-red fox fur was caught on a briar, opossum had left his star-fish shaped tracks in a damp spot, and while I was there a ruffed grouse banged off from a dense raspberry thicket. However, I gradually became aware that some of the paths which I had been following were wide, untidy and full of stripped and trampled canes. I began to wonder who else knew about my berrying woods.

Eventually I came to a falling down sugar shanty. I have always found sugar shanties to be wonderfully interesting places, so I leaned down and looked inside. After my eyes became adjusted to the dimness I was taken aback to see a young bear, of perhaps 80 or 90 pounds, lying in a corner where the winds of countless years had left a comfortable pile of old leaves. He was fast asleep, nose on paws, there in his cool hideaway, conveniently close to all those ripe raspberries, and not far from a beech ridge which would be a pleasant place for the bear in the autumn when the beechnuts ripen. There was a wavy white marking on his chest and he made a few little heaving, grunting noises as he slept, probably dreaming of the lovely days of summertime in the forest.

I quietly withdrew from the sugar house, picked up Lira back at the spring, and we drifted homeward. I was thankful for my noiseless tennis shoes even though I know they are not considered proper wilderness apparel. At last I had seen a wild bear and it had been a fine experience. The bear was safe, content, wild and free in this remote area at the edge of the Folded Hills. I have heard more than one person admit to being lost in this area and I, too, was once quite turned around in here.

God provides for our deepest needs. The needs of the bear for a place where he can range freely, a territory of hills and ravines, fast-flowing streams and quiet backwaters where yellow water lilies grow. And my need to see a wild black bear (*ursus americanus*), for I have always found solace and happiness in the wild folk and wild places of the earth.

Night Life

One of the Psalmists, in a lovely insightful line, wrote, "You made the night and in the darkness all the wild animals come out." This must have been what was happening one July night this summer, long after darkness had set in. There was moonlight, sometimes obscured by drifting clouds, and there were fireflies that served as little blinking torches to help the nocturnal wild folk find their way around. I began to hear a determined rattling and banging of the cat dish that is usually left outside on the fieldstone path by the cabin.

I decided to go out and see if Altoona, my beautiful Persian cat who owns the dish, was hungry. But the dim illumination provided by my flashlight showed someone else, a near-sighted little fellow, a skunk, with the usual black and white color scheme and a really nice plumy tail. This one was somewhere between babyhood and adolescence and he was peering into the cat dish with an expression of disbelief—how could it be so empty? Apparently his dining on some leftover cat food had caused all of the clattering, and he was not old enough to understand that a clean plate is, well, a clean plate! I put a little more food in the bowl in case he returned (he had slipped off into the shrubbery when he noticed me). I was glad I had seen such a fine little animal, who spends a good deal of time cleaning up insects and grubs and really earns his keep, at least if he is treated with cautious respect.

I recalled a time when for several years a mother skunk visited my yard every summer evening. Sometimes she brought her babies with her and they tumbled about her feet and looked trustingly up into my face and gathered happily around the dish of oatmeal and milk I would set out for them. But mostly just the mother skunk came. Her favorite treat was popcorn, fluffy white, fully exploded kernels of that magic corn, touched up with a little butter and salt. We worked our way through a lot of popcorn those summer nights when the fireflies outshone themselves and heat lightning danced fitfully in the far sky. And now another little skunk has brought a touch of wonder to my yard.

I remember reading about a Mr. James Jensen who slowly uncovered the fossil remains of supersaurus, one of the biggest land animals the earth has ever seen, a long-necked dinosaur that weighed about 75 tons and stood as tall as a five story building, a gentle beast, who browsed the high limbs of trees. One moonlit night, Mr. Jensen went to the digging site to look at the bones slowly emerging from the ground for, as he said, "Soft light often reveals shape better than sunlight." And so it is, my little visiting skunk, enveloped by moonlight, shapes up pretty well, a plump little rear end, a thick waving tail, a rather pointed face with mild, worried eyes. He drifts off into the bushes, and what is there to worry about when the quiet mystery of the earth has produced supersaurus, one of the dinosaurs that was here for 140 million years, and a small earnest skunk who lives somewhere near my leafy yard. God dwells steadfastly in the heart of an exploding universe where surprising things are happening. As I return to my cabin and go back to sleep again I recall that Jesus never said too much about sleeping. But he did say, "Watch, then, because you do not know when the Master of the house is coming—it might be in the evening or at midnight or before dawn or at sunrise. If he comes suddenly, he must not find you asleep. What I say to you, then, I say to all: Watch!" (Mark 13:35-37)

Going Down to the Potter's House

Through my writings I have become acquainted with the proprietors of a pottery in Pennsylvania. They are a husband and wife, retired from other careers, and now making handcrafted stoneware, a long-time dream come true. For some time now I have been enjoying a ceramic chickadee bird feeder from this pottery, sent to me as a gift. I have loved the feeder so much that it set me thinking. Christmas shopping can be quite a problem unless I do it in the summertime, for when the stormy days of November and December come, I am often housebound for days. And so I decided that a pottery ware bowl would be a useful and beautiful gift for everyone on my Christmas list. In April I ordered eight identical bowls and in June they came, carefully packed and each one decorated with a familiar, beloved chickadee resting on a green-leaved twig. I set the box away in a closet, secure in the knowledge that so soon I was ready for Christmas!

It is perhaps true that I am a little over-protective of the pottery. The bird feeder has never been entrusted to the great out-of-doors. It is suspended from the ceiling near my writing table where I can see and enjoy it all of the time. In July I gave one of the bowls to clergy friends from the South who vacation every year at a Lake Ontario cottage. An early Christmas remembrance. "Um," Fr. Bruce said appreciatively as he looked the bowl over, "This can be used in the oven." "Oh, don't put it in the oven," I hastily beseeched him. "It says ovenproof on the label that's here with it," he replied. " I wouldn't put it in the oven," I said, alarmed now. My friend went on, calmly reading the label "Re-fired to over 2000 degrees Fahrenheit, Oven-proof, non-toxic and safe to use."

"Oven going to be hotter than 2000 degrees?" he asked. "Well, maybe not," I admitted, while privately thinking that perhaps I am going to have to make visits to all of my friends' homes to see if they are using their bowls properly—properly according to my thinking, that is!

When my potter friends mailed me the bowls they included something for me, a small bead lamp that burns a scented oil. The accompanying note of instructions says that lamps of this design were used in early Greek, Roman and Egyptian cultures. It is decorated with tulip-shaped blue flowers, with a hint of green leafiness. There is a fiberglass wick and a graceful handle that makes it easy to carry the lamp. The potters suggested in the note that "perhaps it will come in handy the next time the lights fail!" Actually, my cabin is "off the electric," so I do not need to wait for a power failure to light my lamp.

Our Lord compared his work of creation to the work of a potter when he said to the prophet Jeremiah, "Go down to the potter's house where I will give you my message." And so Jeremiah went there and saw the potter working at his wheel. Whenever a piece of pottery turned out imperfectly he would take the clay and make it into something else.

Someday I, too, hope to do a little traveling and indeed go down to *this* potter's house, where lovely, serviceable things are turned out, decorated in simple, beautiful ways, with themes copied from the world outside our doors. Deep in my heart I know that I must handle the potter's work with care, loving it with a quiet flame of faith. The creator can remake the clay if that is his wish but I have only one option—to watch carefully over the works of his hands, and care for them with love and perseverance.

Real Blackberry Picking

Last night the beautiful shining full blackberry moon of August almost turned the darkness into daylight. So, with this hint that it is time to begin looking for ripe blackberries, I repair to an abandoned pasture down my old road. I take a little graniteware bucket along to hold the berries. *Real* blackberry pickers are supposed to wear faded blue bib overalls and then tie a small pail to the straps with twine so both hands will be free for picking. They are also supposed to take along milk pails to serve as reservoirs for a large accumulation of berries.

I am not such an intensive picker as that. By the time I have filled my little bucket I am quite scratched up enough, and hot enough, to retreat to a shady spot under the huge maples that grow on the eastern edge of my berry patch. Anyway, milk pails would be a dead giveaway that I had located a heavy-yielding berry patch. Like all real blackberry pickers I can be quite sneaky about the exact site of favorite patches.

It is astonishing what depths of perfidy the innocent occupation of blackberrying can arouse in one. I had an uncle who every summer picked huge quantities of berries back somewhere either on his own farm or perhaps on someone else's farm. Since extracting information from my uncle was a little like questioning the stones at Stonehenge, I worked on his wife, my aunt by marriage. She was a sweet, gentle person who would do all sorts of nice things for you, except set you on the correct sighting to the blackberry patch. With a shrewd, kindly twinkle in her eye she would say, "Oh, they're way back in. Burries [the old-time Northern New York pronunciation] don't amount to much this year. Just enough for a pie." All this when, with your own eyes you had just seen several gallons of dead ripe juicy berries sitting in the cool summer kitchen, ready to be canned, or made into jam, or put into that one lonesome pie.

I, too, am good at doling out sketchy information about blackberries. "I found just enough for supper." "The bushes are all drying up; we need rain bad." Or, "I got turned around finding these. I'd never be able to find the place again." "Turned around" is a countryman's term for being completely lost.

While thinking about all this, I begin to find lovely ripe blackberries that I drop swiftly into my bucket as Lira cleverly nuzzles off many a flavorsome berry to eat on the spot. I discover pathways through the shady thickets indicating that some four-legged picker has also been pleasuring himself with blackberries. These paths are not the delicate trails made by red fox or whitetail deer. They remind me of porcupine's winter pathways in the snow and I am not surprised to find a few long, dark, gleaming porcupine hairs and a few small quills snagged on the bushes. And, after all, why shouldn't porcupine have a generous sampling of the juicy berries, shining like little lumps of coal, from the shady leafy thickets.

A summer would almost seem wasted, for all of us, without blackberries, that lovely harvest of the waning season's hot, drowsy days. Always, somewhere, a feast is spread for those who live in God's world. How nice it is to search for the banquet table and then to share it with others who also love the hills and valleys, woods and streams that mean so much to all of us.

End of Summer

Late August in Northern New York is a time when summer is winding down and every swale and hedgerow is decorated with goldenrod flowers. I have read that in Europe goldenrod has been admitted into gardens and is a cultivated flower, but here in America, perhaps because we have so much of it, we take it more for granted. Anyway, it makes late summer a time of bright gleaming beauty.

Except for the goldfinches, the nesting season is mostly over. Bobolinks have already headed south in their more somber fall plumage, swallows are gathering on the utility lines making plans for a southerly exodus, and chickadees and blue jays are through nesting and are traveling around in small flocks to inspect the pre-autumnal landscape. And so, as I follow a pathway at the meadow's edge near my cabin on August 23rd, I am quite confused to come upon two little bundles of feathers just where I had planned to put my foot down.

Close inspection reveals two little nestling birds, with scalloped gray feathers, bright dark eyes, and quite long bills. They are sitting close together, facing in opposite directions, and seem to be all alone in the world. They watch me with quietude in their eyes, apparently not worried at all that I might step on them or otherwise disarrange their lives. I can't quite think what make of babies these are. The fact that there are just two is suggestive of mourning doves, who ordinarily lay and hatch just two eggs. Still, I have never known them to nest so late in the summer, and nests I have found other years have always been up at about eye level in trees, usually in the fragrant green branches of conifers.

Anyway, after one searching glance, I quietly retreat so as not to agitate the parent birds who must be nearby, or to attract the attention of predators.

Back at home I discover in one of my more obscure reference books that the mourning dove sometimes does nest on the ground. In such a case they do not construct a nest, they simply lay the eggs on the ground. And I begin to notice an adult mourning dove who spends much time sitting on a telephone wire strung across the meadow. She has a brooding air about her and I realize that this is one of the parents keeping watch over the nestlings.

I do not go near the nest again, but day by day check to see if the parent bird is still quietly staying near. For awhile she is always there, perched on the wires. Then for two days in succession, the 28th and the 29th, the adult bird no longer seems to be around. Since the nestlings were quite large and well feathered out, I think probably they have taken wing and left the little spot on the ground that was their first home. I do not go to check this out, knowing that I might have simply failed to look where the parent bird was on the wire.

Then on August 30th I am deeply alarmed to come home from a trip to town to discover that the farmer who tends this land is busily cutting swath after swath of this second growth meadow hay with a haybine, a noisy machine that disposes of the hay in no time at all and would damage the baby birds beyond repair if they were still in the meadow. With a longing, aching heart I hope they have already flown away. I feel it best to wait until the farmer has finally left the field and I have had a chance to shut my dog and cat in the cabin before I go to inspect the location.

With what relief and joy I find that there are no feathers or other signs of demolished birds, just good, sweet fragrant meadow hay. The little birds apparently have been gone for several days, flying off with their parents to the new life that has been awaiting them. With what aching hearts, alarm and anxiety we often regard the treasure we have come to love. We cannot always buy the field where it is located. We just have to love and cherish it and hope that finally all will be gathered up in God's loving hands, for they are stronger and more sure than our own.

Do I not fill heaven and earth? says the Lord.
Jeremiah 23:23

The Blue-Winged Teal

On an early morning walk by the pond in late summer, I almost miss seeing a duck, a lovely little blue-winged teal in eclipse plumage, resting in a sheltered, tiny cove. The sunlight sparkles on the wind-stirred ripples of water and lights up the thick green leaves of the water plantain, growing in all of the pond shallows this summer.

The duck is among floating leaves of this water-loving plant, and so she is almost invisible except to a really inquiring eye. She makes small snuffling calls that sound to me like "wuh, wuh, wuh," and I pass on by so as not to disturb her peace.

I hope no one decides to dredge out the pond, deepening the water and "cleaning out the weeds." Some water plants help to make it a more protected, pleasant

place for the small folk who need a pond and not just a sterile wash basin of water. We humans seem to have an innate longing to clean out and unclog everything we see, including waterways. Some years ago I decided that the tiny springfed brook back of the farmhouse needed cleaning out at a culvert where twigs, leaves and various of nature's cast-offs had slowed up the usual fast flow of water. One bright spring morning I went to work and picked all the sodden debris out of the water. Soon the little brook was singing along, fast and clear again.

And, much to my considerable distress, so were hundreds of tiny black polliwogs, swept along the swift current, through the culvert and out of sight. I was truly dismayed as I knew the polliwogs could not survive in the fast waters, and I hastily started putting the debris back in the stream. I saved many of the little prospective frogs, but I felt very sorry about the damage I had done. I resolved not to do any more stream rehabilitation work, in the near future at least.

At the farmhouse where I once lived I had allowed a great mass of jewelweed, interspersed with catnip, to grow in the back yard. On any summer's day I could sit on the back porch and be accompanied by exquisite, jewel-like hummingbirds who loved these brightly carpeted, flowery pastures.

But eventually it was time for me to move on and the new owners, no doubt regarding these plants as weeds, keep them mowed down. I still regret the loss of this wild garden and at my present home I try to make the yard a place where the hummingbirds can spend happy hours among new flowers.

Sometimes I think we have a tendency to want our earth to be too manicured, too orderly. We are still learning that there is a web of life so intricate and delicate that perhaps we may never truly understand it, and that we need to walk gently on the earth. For the Lord says, "Heaven is my throne and the earth is my footstool" (Isaiah 66:1).

Beautiful words, mysterious words that tell us that the earth belongs to God.

Miracles

Now the misty dreaming days of September have come and it seems that everyone has taken to the road, perhaps to a foliage festival in Maine, or to the nearest u-pick apple orchard, or just to the local cider mill and doughnut shop. Early on a bright fall day I just go on foot to a place back in some wild lands where I once found a cellarhole on a sunny knoll. The dry-stone walls of the cellar had been laid up so carefully and tightly that they are still firm today. A dug well is near the back doorstone and the entire site is covered with garlands of that lovely club moss ground cedar. Ground pine and shining club moss, seem to like best the primeval forest, but I notice that ground cedar loves the old forgotten homesteads found here and there in the Folded Hills.

When I first discovered this place I wandered into a nearby grove of small trees which did not seem to be especially noteworthy until I glanced up and found that they were loaded with small blue plums. Damsons, to be exact. This was really something special, for damsons are not easy to find today. Old-timers loved their tart, spicy flavor and made them up into preserves and sometimes a really elegant plum liqueur that was dispensed in very small quantities to worthy visitors.

Besides being so delicious, damsons have an impressive history. They originated in Syria, near the old city of Damascus. From the Near East they were taken to Italy and on to England by the Roman legions, and finally by the Pilgrims to the New World. Some early settlers in the wild lands took along some damson switches to make their new property seem more homelike. Damson fruits are small, roundish and dark blue. The flesh is firm, yellow, juicy and fairly tart.

I visit the grove every year or so, sometimes finding plums and sometimes not, but it is a fine walk anyway. Today as I approach the old home place, the breeze is sending down a sifting of faded rosy plum leaves. Up in the tree are two raccoons. Their hind legs are braced on the small branches, and they are leaning into the plums, using their front paws to shovel in the little fruits. They

69

are so busy that they do not notice our arrival until I step on a dry twig. Then they turn and regard us with their bright, beaming, inquisitive eyes, trying to decide if we are trouble.

Watching the two black-masked "little bears" I thought of a friend with whom I had been discussing raccoons one day. I had been telling her about the raccoon babies born in my hollow maple tree and how really nice it was at dusk to see them cautiously backing down the tree trunk. The mother then hurried down headfirst and they would all disappear into the darkness. My friend said "Raccoons make a dreadful mess of my garbage!" Well, maybe, but had she ever seen them up in a damson tree, their faces framed by ripe blue plums?

Lira is at an age when she is not much interested in bothering raccoons, so we sat down in the shade and rested awhile. Eventually the raccoons climbed down and went rolling off along an old wagon track, snuffing and sniffling and bumping companionably into each other, probably heading toward their den tree and a good day's sleep.

Then I had my turn and gathered a kettle of plums. That same day the plums were cooked down into jam on my wood stove, bringing all the delicate flavor of fall into the cabin.

Some people told Jesus, "Teacher, we want to see you perform a miracle." I am not sure just what they required, but I think that miracles are not all that hard to find.

Walking in the Light

Late one September afternoon I happened to see a pheasant casually walking across the old road near my cabin. He stepped down a roadside bank, heavily shrubbed with wild raspberry bushes (bearing a late second bed with wild raspberry bushes (bearing a late second crop of berries) and walked into an open meadow south of the road. All summer I had not seen a pheasant, although there had probably been nests in the nearby ungrazed woodlands, along the edges of the marshy swales and brushy hedgerows. Somehow the pheasants had all kept out of sight. Now in September, dangerously close to the hunting season, they had become visible. This is apt to happen every year at about this time whether they have nested locally or are from stock released sometime during the summer. Perhaps autumn brings out the wanderlust in the birds and they want to step out unafraid and handsome, part of the bright palette of the season's colors.

Several days later while driving down the old road late one hushed fall afternoon, I saw three pheasants emerge from beneath a canopy of grapevines in a hedgerow along one side of the wild strawberry meadow. The grape leaves, an almost transparent pale yellow now, brought a gentle glow of brightness to that part of the meadow. Sometimes a little stirring of the air would cause a few to float softly to the ground, as if in benediction for the waning days of warm weather.

The pheasants moved into a patch of frosted red clover where they warily watched my car, which I had brought to a halt, and I watched the pheasants. There were two males, with the usual flashy pheasant coloring, a daub of crimson beneath each eye, a perfect match really for the lovely deep glowing red of a maple leaf that I had just picked up along the road. I wondered if Joseph's coat of many colors, that got him into so much trouble, was any finer than the colors adorning the little meadow. I remembered my grocery clerk friend who only that morning had remarked to me that the autumn colors must be so beautiful now "up north." She longed to take to the open road searching for the places where the color was peaking.

71

Besides the two males there was a little brown female and I lost sight of her now and then as she moved about in the frost-browned clover. The three of them would all crouch down a bit from time to time and move about in the grasses. When they did this I could never see them even though the clover wasn't very high and the males were so brilliantly colored. There is some legerdemain involved here during these beautiful, misty, dreaming days of autumn.

This must be one way the pheasants keep the hunters off-base during the hunting season. While the hunter is wasting his time and shot in one place, the pheasant is crouching and running fast to some little brushy island of safety. He also seems to mark special sanctuaries such as straw stacks, hay bales left in the fields, and even farm buildings where he can hide for awhile.

For all their flamboyant appearance, these birds are so skillful at hiding that once the season opens and the guns begin to roar they become so elusive that after the first few days hunters often tire of the chase. And so, if all goes well, these lovely birds I watch should have a good winter with plenty to eat. Endless acres of corn are grown in this area, mostly harvested and processed as high moisture corn. Many of the golden kernels are spilled on the ground and are consumed all winter by deer, opossums, foxes, pheasants and other wildlife.

I start up my car and drive on, watched with curiosity by the pheasants, all part of the lovely painted-leaf moon of autumn.

You yourselves used to be in the darkness, but since you have become the Lord's people, you are in the light. So you must live like people who belong to the light, for it is the light that brings a rich harvest of every kind of goodness, righteousness, and truth.

Ephesians 5:8-9

Keeping Busy

For many years I have taken an old-fashioned gray graniteware kettle with me on my walks. This provides my excuse for being abroad, depending upon the season of the year. For, as Henry David Thoreau noted, people are likely to have suspicions of someone who is just wandering around, seemingly not working. We have trouble relinquishing the role of Martha in this world, or indeed seeing others relinquish it. And who am I to speak; I love a loaf of new-baked bread, a clean kitchen floor, a simmering kettle of soup as well as the next one.

Anyway, my kettle is my defense against being regarded as an idler. For anyone can plainly see those lovely windfall apples clearly destined for applesauce or perhaps an apple crisp, or the scissors to snip off the especially mild, juicy wild grapes that I have found. There is really nothing so good as wild grape jelly poured into sparkling clean jars and tucked away in the old wooden cupboard, or perhaps grape jelly tempered to a more gentle, delicate flavor and lighter color by adding some apple juice to the jelly kettle. Then all summer long there are berries to pick—wild strawberries, red raspberries, blackcaps and blackberries. Or perhaps it is early autumn and I invade the little marshes along the creek to pull up some roots of *apios americana* (groundnut). It is not easy to find these roots down in the murky bog, but once I have found them and dragged them to the surface, I can snip off innumerable starchy little tubers that boil up in 10 or 12 minutes, and garnished with butter, pepper and salt make a delightful, "little potato," with a nut-like flavor, for the noontime lunch.

In early spring, I follow my wild asparagus trail and am usually able to find enough tender young spears for a meal mostly of asparagus, one of my very favorite vegetables. Along the creek I can pick up small pieces of sun-bleached, dried driftwood that burn with a lovely glow in my little woodstove. In the fall, I just might come across a giant puffball exuding a fragrance reminiscent of its earthy origins—fallen nuts and wood smoke and the fading of summer into a new season. Sliced up and fried with a little butter they are a wonderful autumn food. After the first frosts, that loosen up the beechnut burs, I go back to the beech ridges in the deep woods and fight over the nuts with the jays and squirrels. It isn't much of a fight, for the jays and squirrels, as well as the partridges, deer, bears, foxes, opossums, raccoons and so on, are always way out front in the race to collect the much-admired nuts. But if I poke around a bit in the fallen pale bronze beech leaves I can almost always find enough to fill the little salt bag that I like to put them in. The sweet beechnuts are just great to see in turkey or chicken stuffing for the Thanksgiving dinner that will be coming up soon.

And so it goes. Even in winter, I can pick up solid pieces of fallen branch wood that will put a dancing aliveness in my wood fires. From the banquet going on now and forevermore in God's kingdom, I fill my kettle with the lovely leftovers that make life an unending song of praise to him

Jesus took the five loaves and two fish, looked up to heaven, thanked God for them, broke them, and gave them to the disciples to distribute to the people. They all ate and had enough, and the disciples took up twelve baskets of what was left over.

Luke 9:16-17

Apple Butter

One autumn day when I was having lunch with a friend and her family, she placed a jar of freshly made apple

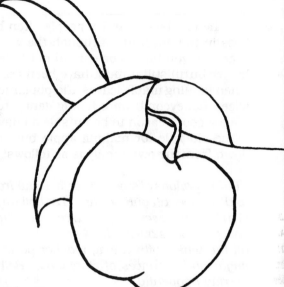

butter proudly
on the table in
front of me
and said, "I'm
so glad you're
here. I just
love to make
apple butter,
but my family
won't eat it
and I know
you like it." I
was pleased to
be able to par-
take of this
fine autumnal
food and also
glad that I had at least
one useful function in the world, as an appreciative
consumer of apple butter. Apparently apple butter is
something you either love or you don't. I remember that
Della Lutes, a country writer earlier in this century,
remarked that she and her father both had a low opinion
of apple butter. Her father thought it tasted like green
wood chips stewed up in molasses. Nevertheless, I regard
apple butter as a delightful product of the autumn pre-
serving kettles.

My first introduction to this delicacy was in early childhood when my mother bought a jar from the A & P Tea
Company man who had a weekly route past our Lake
Ontario farm in the '30s and early '40s. At the same time
she bought a round loaf of a steamed brown bread that
the A & P carried. It was rich and moist and full of the
lovely, gummy, sticky, raisins that so enhanced almost
any bakery product of those days. Spread with thick,
spicy apple butter it seemed a heavenly food, to put it
mildly.

In the old days, country people often had apple butter bees in the autumn. Although the work was hard and exacting (you had to be careful not to let the thickening butter burn) still it must have been really nice on a day when flaming maple leaves and poplar leaves the color of sliced honeycomb were falling gently to the ground, to have a good reason to be outside all day.

One old rule for making apple butter that has come down from my own family is as follows:

Put 10 gallons of sweet cider in a cauldron (copper or iron) and set over an outdoor fire. Let boil down to half. Then slowly add 3 pecks of pared, cored and quartered apples. Let cook over slow fire for 4 or 5 hours. Then add, stirring all the while with a long washer paddle, 10 pounds of sugar and 5 ounces of cinnamon. Boil until thickened, stirring frequently.

I think my friend makes hers in smaller quantities on the electric range. The whole house takes on the delicate flavor of fall, and there is a good sense of security in knowing that someone has gone to the trouble to make apple butter.

Speak to the earth, and it shall teach thee.

                                                      Job 12:8

The Pear Tree

In the autumn when the sky is an untroubled pure blue and the color is luring my neighbors to the Catskills, the Adirondacks, Vermont, or the Canadian Laurentians, my thoughts often turn to pears, lovely fruit that graces all the roadside marketing stands now. For I dearly love them, especially homegrown ones. Pears that have been touched by gentle breezes, ripened by the warm sun-shine, cooled by fresh drops of rain, and that have finally dropped from the tree with little sighing thuds to lie in the long, soft orchard grasses.

One of my favorite mentors, Henry David Thoreau, did not seem to share my love for pears. He wrote in one of his journals that "Pears are a less poetic though more aristo-cratic fruit than apples. They have neither the beauty nor the fragrance of apples, but their excellence is in their flavor. . ." He adds, rather grumpily, "They are named after emperors, kings, queens, dukes and duchesses. I fear I shall have to wait till we get to pears with American names which a republican can swallow." Umm, well, in a ponderous book on pears which I located in the library I did find quite a few that had been named after royalty, but I found some with names that I am sure would have appealed to Thoreau—the Shakespeare (a little sugar pear), the Lincoln, the Vermont Beauty and the New Meadow to mention just a few.

When we first moved to our town of Rodman farm in 1959 it was springtime, the beautiful flowering month of May. Before long I discovered an abandoned cellarhole down our old road, surrounded by lilacs and little old-fashioned pink rosebushes. Standing by itself, a short distance away, was a pear tree in full bloom, with a drift of snowy white flowers that did seem to hint of noble, aristocratic places—perhaps the lovely lost palace of Fontainebleau, or maybe Windsor Castle. Here was a treasure that I would check on many times through quite a few summers. Every year the tree bore a bountiful crop of what were probably bartlett pears. They were large and yellow with a glow of russet red on one side. When fully ripe they were very tender pears, melting in your mouth, dripping juice through your fingers. But this did not matter; the best place to eat a sun-ripened pear anyway is under the tree where it has grown.

Unfortunately, I was not able to harvest too many of

these pears myself, for I soon discovered that the inhabitants of almost the entire countryside had this pear tree on their minds. Knowledge of its location seemed universal. I fended off all kinds of neighborly inquiries about the tree, hoping to distract attention from it, all to no avail. For years the harvest had been appropriated by "all sorts and conditions" of people.

That first year, however, I felt that since I lived so close to the gracious, elegant pear tree I could surely make a clean sweep of the fruits before others aroused themselves and hastened to gather the pears. I was wrong, and over the ensuing years I was seldom able to garner more than two or three pears every autumn—perhaps a pear still on the tree, hidden by a little clump of leaves, or one or two that had rolled off in the grass where they had been overlooked. Even a little russet-brown woodchuck, busy storing up his autumnal layer of fat, whom I saw one day furtively slipping through the tall grasses beneath the tree, seemed to have better luck than I did. For he found an especially fine pear that he carefully held in his bony black fingers while biting into its juicy goodness.

The successful harvesters never seemed to sleep and they never lost sight of their quarry. They usually walked in from the other end of the old road, where there were no houses, as further concealment of their traffic in pears. People might freely discuss the pear tree in winter, spring and summer, and also late fall; but in early fall was not the time for talk. Then it was that the populace made visits to the tree in as clandestine a manner as though they were journeying to a concealed still down some old woods' road.

But as long as I knew the tree was there I did not mind too much. I could always hope and dream about the baskets full of pears that someday I would claim for my own. Unfortunately, this dream was never realized. For one year in early autumn some rather heedless farm boys who lived in the neighborhood came by. They had sacks and baskets and told me they were going to "get them pears." Well, they not only got the pears, they got the tree, too. When next I saw it, the lovely tree was a trashed wreck. Instead of carefully picking the fruits or gently shaking the boughs, the boys had simply broken down the branches that the fruit might be more easily picked. The poor tree was ruined. I sorrowed over this for a long time. Indeed I still do. The only comfort I can get from this episode is that a high regard for pear trees was put into my heart and some day, remembering that beloved tree, I will plant another pear tree in my garden, on my own land, where I can protect and care for it with my own hands.

. . .the fruit of the earth shall be excellent and comely.
Isaiah 4:2

Looking for a Friend

Back on the hillside last night I heard the sharp bark of a fox and I was glad to think of a little fox, safe in the edge of the Folded Hills, having a word or two (fox language) about this lovely autumn time. It is hard for a small fox to keep totally quiet in the lovely changing season of autumn, when the fierce wild grapes he loves hang heavily on the vines and the windfall apples are plentiful. Actually, foxes usually let the apples freeze a few times in late fall and early winter before feeding on them regularly. Perhaps this is because there is so much other food now—the grapes, the late wild raspberries, and mice, crickets and grasshoppers. Possibly the frosts mellow the apples so their taste becomes more appealing.

I never see as much of fox as I would like to. On summer mornings I sometimes see his neat straight tracks in the early morning dew that lies on the fields, before the sun has erased this fragile trail. In winter I find his tracks in the snow and sometimes there are strange little caches along the trails where he has tucked away bits of food for days when the hunting may be poor and a little fox stomach is feeling pinched and empty. He digs down a bit in the snow or dirt and deposits perhaps a meadow mouse or a bit of a partridge or part of an unfortunate bunny. Then he covers this treasure over with whatever is handy, perhaps dead leaves, withered grasses or twigs. I am sorry to say that Lira, who does not really need extra food, has been known to dig down and ransack these little storage pits. Besides losing his food to my freeloading dog, the little wild one may sometimes lose his dinner in even stranger ways. I once found tracks in the snow that showed where a fox had caught a cottontail and was smugly trotting off with it when a great horned owl swooped down and effortlessly relieved fox of his burden, leaving his mighty marks and a feather or two behind in the snow. A little mixed up maze of tracks indicated that the fox had at first trotted aimlessly around in astonished confusion before finally tracking off supperless through the heavy snow.

Foxes are related to dogs. They both belong to the order *canidae*, but way back in the mists of time someone discovered that the ancestor of our modern dogs had a shy sense of companionship with humans and could be induced to share with them the crude comforts of the flickering campfires, the caves, the excitement of the hunt, and could be taught to live and guard and trust his people.

Foxes have a wariness and a wilderness, but like dogs they have a sense of fun and love and perhaps a little lonesomeness deep in their heart.

One time I quietly watched as a red fox trotted into a small barn near my old farmhouse. He sniffed about and cocked his ears and finally picked up a bit of ancient leather horse harness from a cobwebby corner of the barn. He tossed it up into the air once, catching it as it fell toward the floor, and then trotted off towards the hills, carrying the find in his mouth. He acted exactly like my dog does when she is sometimes seized by a spirit of playfulness and tosses one of my mittens up into the air, catches it and runs around, wanting me to chase her and try to get the mitten back.

I think the fox had babies back in some overgrown pasture hillside and felt they needed something to tug on and play with, and why wouldn't a nice piece of old harness be just the thing, still smelling no doubt, at least to a keen fox nose, of big sweaty work horses and hay barns and oat bins?

A few years ago, Lira spied a fox one day in a nearby meadow and gave chase to it, barking loudly and menacingly. The fox skimmed lightly off over the snow leaving Lira far behind, then, his thick reddish-gold fur gleaming in the cold wintry sunshine, sat down in the snow and barked encouragingly at Lira. This set Lira off again, but she eventually panted her way back to the fireside without coming even close to the fox.

Somehow, from this unpromising beginning, they became good friends. And often, for several years, I would see a glint of wild reddish fur in some hedgerow, along a roadside or perhaps on the edge of the pines, and Lira would rush to greet this friend, wagging her tail in a pleased way. The fox would stand and watch her with a guarded, uncertain look; but you could see a touch of shy gladness in his eyes as he watched this friend from another world, a settled protected world. After a moment or two the fox would slip away and Lira would return to my side.

Early one morning when Lira was still in the house but I was out in the cold gray light of an early winter's morning trying to start my car, the fox came pattering over the icy, frozen fields. He stopped some distance from the house and barked several times, watching hopefully to see if he could arouse his friend. I wished I could go to the house and let Lira out, but I knew that if I made any movement at all the fox would bound away in alarm. So I could only stand and watch as he finally gave up, and in a disappointed way resumed his travelings, perhaps back to the hillside where he often beds down for the day beneath some thick spruces which provide good protection from the harsh winds and driving snows of our northern winters.

There is a lonely quality to a fox as he travels with the wind along the ridge tops, down by streams and across the frozen ponds and marshes. But he does have the beautiful earth God gave him and now and then a special friend.

And so I walk in the presence of the Lord in the world of the living.

Psalm 116:9

All About Bluebirds

October is a month of blazing color, for Jack Frost has been abroad in the land. Modern botanists discounted this method of leaf coloring, but I am sure it was Jack Frost I saw out in the old maple tree last night giving a final touch of brassy gold to the leaves. Amid all of this glory I see eight bluebirds down the old pasture lane. Friendly little birds of dooryard and garden, but not seen so often now, for their hold on life is uncertain. There is the lovely sky-blue back, the rusty-red breast and the shining white feathers. They sit on the fenceposts and occasionally one will drop to the ground and snap up an insect. After awhile they go roller-coasting off to a dead elm tree and perch on its branches. Finally they fly off through the golden grandeur of this autumn day. Probably they are on the move southward. Bluebirds migrate during the daytime, unlike many birds who prefer the night. Even though my bluebird sightings are years apart now, still it seems that I have always known them. Perhaps this goes back to my childhood in the champion hills. We had two transparent apple trees near the wellhouse, and every spring bluebirds nested in them, finding small hollows that suited their needs. The transparent is a hardy, yellow apple that originated in Russia when Cossacks and wolves disputed the territory and an apple tree had to stand some real teeth-chattering weather. Every year in August the transparents dropped a bountiful crop of early, well flavored apples in the long grass beneath the trees. Since even the late, late keepers such as the russets had long given out, we were hungry for fresh apples to eat out of hand and cook up into applesauce. I don't recall that we used transparents too much for apple pie, but when they had ripened we knew that the duchess apples (another hardy Russian import) would soon be ready for picking, and there is nothing quite like the first duchess apple pie of the season.

However far away any of us might wander, down through the years, we always remembered with affection the transparent trees. The bluebirds also remembered and never failed to return there when spring reclaimed the northlands.

Bluebirds and apple trees just seem to go together. A nearby pasture is desirable, for the bluebird likes to pick up grasshoppers, crickets, beetles, cutworms and caterpillars. A yard or garden are also good feeding places for them. Several years ago I hopefully put up a bluebird box on a fence post near my cabin. Each year chickadees and tree swallows look it over but finally go elsewhere to nest, leaving wrens in possession. The wrens stuff the box full of twiggy material, innocently calling attention to their efforts with bubbling cascades of song. However, wrens make any number of bogus nests and I do not know if they actually raise their babies there or not.

83

During early spring and late fall, when insects are scarce, bluebirds enjoy small wild fruits and bittersweet berries. Since there is a good supply of these foods on my land I hope that someday bluebirds will find the nest box. It would be good to be near a bluebird nest again—the clutch of pale blue eggs, then the fledglings, winsome little birds with thrush spotting and bluish-gray coloring. Maybe I could plant a few transparent apple trees and really bring the bluebirds back again!

Teach Us to Pray

Several years ago Halloween was fast approaching and, as seems quite appropriate for that holiday, a black cat arrived at my home. I first saw it in the garage, a young cat four or five months old, coal black with grave, pale yellow eyes. There was a ragged little stump of a tail, perhaps the result of some Manx genes, which are not uncommon around here. He hid beneath the car when he saw me, peeking out hopefully though, just in case I happened to have anything I was planning to offer him to eat. "Please, God," I breathed worriedly, "please keep this cat going. You know I have more than I can handle now and I just can't take care of anything more. Please, God, don't let him stay."

Well, somewhere on its way to heaven, this prayer got short-circuited, for the farm turned out to be the cat's chosen home. I learned to love him and named him October for the month in which he came. I set out dishes of cat food and milk for him in the garage or barn, and on cold winter nights I put him down in the warm cellar for his nighttime schedule of sleep, mouse hunting, etc. His favorite place to sleep was stretched out on top of one of the furnace's hot air pipes. I bought him distemper and rabies shots and had him altered so that he would not get hurt in fights with other cats.

When spring and summer came, I found that although he was an affectionate, loving cat, still in some ways he was a hermit at heart and would spend several days at a time "camping out," as I called it. I would catch glimpses of him in the meadows and woods, along the old road, or near the two camps that are located some distance down the road. Then he would come home, hungry and wistful looking. I would feed him and then hold him for awhile, stroking his sleek black fur while he purred like a little engine on idle.

Then a sober look always came into his eyes. I imagine it was the same sort of look that came into the eyes of the man who first heard the news about gold at Sutter's Mill. Other places were calling and I knew that in a short while he would be scampering off down the old road and out of sight. I did not worry too much as I knew that he caught plump field mice and could do most of his own providing in the summertime.

This general schedule went on for several years. The colder months were spent at the farmstead and during the warmer season he mostly "tented out," coming home every few days when he felt lonesome and hungry.

Then came a time when the days stretched into weeks and the weeks into months, and I did not see a sign of my beloved cat with the soft, shiny black fur and the lovely humming purr. Whenever I went to the spring for water or down the old road near the cabin, I called and called to him. I crawled under porches, searched the barns and all sorts of obscure places. After he had been absent three months I telephoned all the neighbors, asking them to be on the lookout for a black cat with a funny tail. They were sympathetic and promised to help, and told me many lost-cat stories of their own, but there was no ringing telephone to bring me good news.

By now I was sure that October must have died. I hoped

85

that it had not been a hard way to die. I imagined all sorts of events: his limp little body being carried off by a dog, coyote or wolf; his being held in a trap until he died of injuries; that he was stolen and sold to a research laboratory; being shot. And so it went. "Please God," I would whisper in my heart, "Please keep him safe. Please bring him back home."

One sunny day in September I saw what seemed to be a black speck in a far field. I did not dare to hope too much. I had been fooled before, mostly by crows, once by a neighbor's cat, and several times by woodchucks. However, I watched and whatever it was seemed to be coming slowly toward the farmhouse. I began calling and the movement speeded up a little. Then I started running to meet him, for I was sure by now that it was October. It was a good thing I ran to meet him because he was exhausted and could barely move when I finally picked him up and held him in my arms. I carried him home, and after several days of food and rest he was back in shape once more, but he did not go camping again that fall. I never knew what happened to him in the long interlude when he was missing, but "Thank you so much, God, for sorting out my prayers and answering them—the last prayers, I mean. He is so very dear to me."

If you believe, you will receive whatever you ask for in prayer.

Matthew 21:22

Voices of Autumn

When I went outside on a morning in late October, there was a gauzy autumn mist almost everywhere. Now is the time when the color is fading into a gentle, lingering beauty. Willow brush in the swale has leaves of the very palest yellow now and traces of red and midas gold still brighten the maples, but mostly their leaves are on the ground beneath the trees which are preparing for the stark, almost ominous season of winter.

This is the time for many enchanting little out-of-season resurgences of springtime when all was new beginnings, warm sunshine and exuberant birdsong. Did I think the dandelions were all gone for this year? I was wrong, for here is one just where I had almost stepped, and I turn aside to admire this moist golden flower, really special now that it is just about the only one around. And then there are the voices of autumn. A few spring peepers call from the pond, skimmed over now with rusty-gold elm leaves and the pale gold of tender, faded, black cherry leaves. In springtime the lovely piercing whistled notes of the white-throated sparrow come from all the trees and brushy places. Now I hear just one of these messages from "Old-sam-peabody-peabody-peabody" coming from somewhere in the hedgerow behind my cabin. The bushes are a little threadbare now but they still provide a good place for the white-throats to rummage around in on their way southward. Sometimes a subdued "o-ka-lee" reminds me of the day in March when the red-winged blackbirds regained noisy possession of their northern marshlands.

From a moist seephole in the small meadow I hear a call that restlessly stirs my memory, but not quite enough to recognize it at first. So beautiful and so well-remembered, if I could just think what bird produces that unusual song.

Finally a springtime scene comes to my mind, a cold raw day in late March or early April when I hear a peremptory, harsh "beep" coming from the wetlands as the sun sinks towards the horizon. This is always spring for me, regardless of the calendar, for it is the woodcock come back to his vernal singing grounds.

I live right about in the middle of a good singing ground (I had a friend who asked me once if I didn't miss musical concerts living way out here in the country!) so gradually I hear these "beeps" in a vast circle all around me. Then one of the strange little birds flies skyward in an upward spiral making a beautiful twittering noise with his wings as he goes. Hundreds of feet into the air he begins to circle, calling his marvelous courting song, a fluidly lovely "tu-tu-tu-tu" that welds the earth and sky into one. Finally, the little bird with springtime in his heart and voice zig-zags down to the ground and all is quiet for a short time until his nasal "beep" begins again. This is the song I am hearing now in the misty meadows of autumn, a farewell to his lovely northern habitat where he ushered in spring on nights of cold, snow, fog, and rain—although he especially loved moonlit nights when his tireless flights might go on almost until dawn.

I remember a friend who remarked during the summer that she had seen the strangest bird in her yard; it had long legs and looked like a chipmunk. This seemed like a truly astonishing bird description to me and I remembered an essay, "Sharp Eyes," by the naturalist John Burroughs, in which he wrote, "Persons frequently describe to me some bird they have seen or heard and ask me to name it, but in most cases the bird might be any one of a dozen, or else is totally unlike any bird found on this continent." I am afraid I was not much help, but eventually my friend reported that a relative who is a forest ranger identified it as an American woodcock. "Really!" I replied in a somewhat stupefied way, for I never would have said that a woodcock resembled a chipmunk on long legs. I went home, still baffled, and hunted up a picture of the woodcock in one of my bird books. My friend had a point after all, for there is a soft drift of stripes through a woodcock's feathers that could remind one of a chipmunk. However, its legs are short and rather weak, at least in appearance, for such a plump, chunky little bird.

Perhaps it was a snipe which she saw. This also has a striped effect on the back and head and does have long legs. Neither is exactly a yard bird, but my friends' house is near a boggy area with streams and I imagine it would not be impossible for either one to show up on her lawn.

My own glimpses of woodcock, after the nesting season is over, are usually on the pathways along the edge of nearby pine plantations. The pine seem to be well regarded by the little birds with the outsize bills, the huge dark eyes, and the feathers in lovely earthen shades of russet, brown and black.

And now he sings this quietly joyful song of good-bye to the northern lands that he loves especially well in the very early spring when climactic conditions can be rough; but who cares, for these are the *singing grounds*!

Send your light and your truth;
May they lead me
And bring me back to Zion,
Your sacred hill,
And to your Temple, where you live.
Then I will go to your altar, O God;
You are the source of my happiness.
I will play my harp and sing praise to you
O God, my God.

Psalm 43:3-4

Trail of Springs

One of my treasures is a small, old, tin folding cup that I always carry with me on my walks. The cup is very useful, for I have a trail of springs and when I come to one of them I unfold the cup and dip it into the living waters for a cool drink. No matter what direction I take I will pass near a spring. I do not have to wait for Moses to strike a rock and bring forth water, for this is Great Lakes country and long ago God's hand supplied us with innumerable streams, springs, waterfalls, bogs, and waterholes.

There is the little spring under a maple tree on the pasture hillside. It is surrounded by a low fieldstone wall and where the water bubbles up through the light gravelly sand, I once found a small, round, dusky-red stone with a hole in the center. I think it is a bead from an Indian necklace and it is nice to think of the bright-eyed native Americans knowing and using this spring that I love. Now when I visit it in the season of autumn mists and silence I just find a few peach-golden maple leaves floating on the water.

Another ever-flowing spring is probably known only to me, for the waters pour out from beneath sprawling branches of a large elderberry bush. They go directly into a little feeder brook near my cabin. The elderberries are always large and juicy because the roots never have to scrounge for water.

Behind a cellarhole down the old road there was always a seepage of water from beneath the roots of an old apple tree. Sometimes I dug down just a bit and the water always bubbled up faster. It was a beautiful place. In May pink and white apple blossom petals fell where the spring emerged. In late summer fragrant red apples streaked with yellow tumbled down onto the bright green grass that revealed the presence of underground water.

This probably had been the water supply for the farmhouse that once stood here. After years of disuse the spring had become silted in. A camp was built nearby and drinking water was needed, so I mentioned this spring to the owners. I usually do not "go public" about my trail of springs. A backhoe was used to dig out and enlarge the spring and a lovely flood of freely flowing water emerged. A heavy cement enclosure was set down over the spring and an overflow pipe carries the water down to the camp where it continually flows into an old iron trough.

90

Another spring that I like to visit pours its water out from beneath some solid shelving rocks and then on into the "big creek." The waters are hidden, for a thriving clump of wild mint screens their place of emergence. I learned about the location of this spring on a sweltering summer's day, when the waters of the creek, flowing over a streambed of flat rock, had become almost lukewarm. A wedge of about thirty brook trout had arranged themselves in the current of new water from the spring, as it flowed into and finally mingled with the tepid creek waters. I watched the fish, olive-brown on top, with reddish-orange fins, gently moving with the flowing water, and realized that brook trout aren't even supposed to *be* in this stream. It is not stocked with fish and according to local wisdom is "fished out." But here they were in all their beauty, revealing the presence of the hidden spring to any passer-by. Trout can be depended upon to find and make good use of a springhole.

I like to think of others who came before me and used the little tin cup, a relic of older days, to dip up living waters when they were thirsty. Nothing is as satisfying as clear, cold water in the heat of the day.

Let him that is athirst come. And whosoever will, let him take the water of life freely.

Rev. 22:17